One Two Three

一二三

孙永合◎著

Copyright © 2022 Yonghe Sun（孙永合）

ISBN：978-1-957144252

All right reserved. 版权所有

No part of this publication may be reproduced distributed, or transmitted in any form or by means, including photocopying, recording, or other electronic or mechanical methods, without the prior written permission of the publisher, except in the case of brief quotations embodied in critical reviews and certain other noncommercial uses permitted by copyright law. For permission requests, write to the author, addressed "Attention: Permissions Coordinator" at

syhe666@163.com

本书由美国 Asian Culture Press 出版

Published by Asian Culture Press

1942 Broadway, Suite 314C

Boulder, CO 80302, United States

Web: https://www.asianculture.press

Translated by Diana Leng

Published in the United States of America

First paperback edition May 2022

本书 2022 年 5 月在美国第一次出版

《一二三》简介

　　《一二三》共 5 章，分别由 11，22，33，44 和 13 篇组成，共 123 篇，969 句。其中最短篇 39 字，最长篇 123 字，正文约 12000 字。它采用和发扬了三字经的形式，每句基本上分为上下两半句，共 12 字。每篇标题为三个字，大多数以第一句前三字为标题，少数以前三句头一字组合成标题，极少数以其中或最后三字为标题。

　　《一二三》吸收了中国文化的精华，如成语，诗句，常用语等，以吃穿住行能，安康福乐寿，真正创善美为主要中心思想，进行逐步论述，力求做到短小精炼，实用易懂，最终达到传承创新中国文化和推动世界和平发展的目标。如果这本书能够得到您的认可，或对您有所帮助，那将是作者最大的愿望！

作者简介

孙永合，中国河北威县侯贯镇西董吕庄人，生于1966年，84年初中毕业，87年在威县和衡水京大路帮二姐家开汽车配件，约89年在威县章台镇自家开汽车农机配件，至今未变。多年来他利用业余时间，总结了中国的一些优秀文化，并结合自己的亲身经历，认真思考，终于完成了这本三字经形式的《一二三》，希望大家多提意见和建议，以便进一步改进和完善。可以在今日头条中搜索"真正创善美"，给他发私信，在此作者谢谢您啦。

地址：中国河北省威县章台镇。

目录

Chapter 1

(1) Heaven, Earth, and Man (001) 2
(2) You, I, and It (002) 2
(3) Yesterday, Today, and Tomorrow (003) 2
(4) Food, Clothing, and Shelter (004) 3
(5) Safety, Health, and Fortune (005) 3
(6) True Creation (006) 3
(7) Fake Crooked Fee (007) 4
(8) Danger, Sickness, and Death (008) 4
(9) Thousands of Years (009) 4
(10) The Creation of Chinese Characters (010) 5
(11) The East is Bright (011) 5

Chapter 2

(1) One, Two, Three (012) 8
(2) Derived from Blue (013) 8
(3) Dialectical Laws (014) 9
(4) The Three Ends of the Object (015) 9
(5) Observe First (016) 10
(6) Knowing that This Is the Way It Is (017) 10
(7) Continuous Time (018) 11
(8) Indirect Exchange (019) 11
(9) Temperature, Water, and Substances (020) 12
(10) Worldview (021) 12
(11) Motion Produces Exchange (022) 13
(12) Human Heredity (023) 13

(13) A Man Itself (024) ……………………………………………………………… 14
(14) Private and Public (025) ……………………………………………………… 14
(15) Administering Benevolent Rule (026) ……………………………… 15
(16) All Things Grow (027) ………………………………………………………… 15
(17) All things (028) ………………………………………………………………… 16
(18) Creation of the system (029) ……………………………………………… 16
(19) Leave the Landscape (030) ………………………………………………… 17
(20) Leave Intelligence (031) …………………………………………………… 17
(21) Wishing to Get (032) ………………………………………………………… 18
(22) Starting From (033) ………………………………………………………… 18

Chapter 3

(1) Gold, Wood and Water (034) ……………………………………………… 20
(2) No Food and Clothing (035) ………………………………………………… 20
(3) What's the Thing (036) ……………………………………………………… 21
(4) Crossing the Mountain In Front (037) ………………………… 21
(5) A Life of Ease (038) ………………………………………………………… 22
(6) Starting from Together (039) …………………………………………… 22
(7) Diabetic Patients (040) ……………………………………………………… 23
(8) Too Much Carelessness (041) …………………………………………… 23
(9) Poor Health (042) ……………………………………………………………… 24
(10) In the Face of Crisis (043) ……………………………………………… 24
(11) Grass on the Wall (044) …………………………………………………… 25
(12) Facing a Deep Stream (045) ……………………………………………… 25
(13) Where Do I Come From (046) …………………………………………… 26
(14) Good Education (047) ………………………………………………………… 26
(15) Ancient Heroes (048) ………………………………………………………… 27
(16) Traveling a Thousand Miles (049) …………………………………… 27
(17) The Spirit of Equanimity (050) ……………………………………… 28
(18) The Polite Manner (051) …………………………………………………… 28
(19) You Have the Love (052) …………………………………………………… 29
(20) The Hustle and Bustle of the World (053) ………………… 29
(21) The Human Spirit (054) ……………………………………………………… 29
(22) Having Vitality (055) ………………………………………………………… 29
(23) Food, Oil, and Vegetables (056) …………………………………… 30
(24) Nourishing the Body (057) ………………………………………………… 30
(25) Guan Guan Dove (058) ………………………………………………………… 31
(26) Gentleman's Friendship (059) …………………………………………… 31
(27) Dear Brothers (060) …………………………………………………………… 32

(28) Knowing Obviously (061) 32
(29) Going South in Wrong Direction (062) 33
(30) Looking Back (063) 33
(31) The Unintentionally Planted Willow (064) 34
(32) My Hometown (065) 34
(33) The Internet (066) 35

Chapter 4

(1) The Creation of Infinite Beauty (067) 38
(2) The Way of The Great Learning (068) 38
(3) Focus on Time and Direction (069) 39
(4) More or Less (070) 39
(5) In the Jungle (071) 40
(6) The Bear's Paw and the Fish (072) 41
(7) The Foundation of the Object (073) 41
(8) The Meaning of the Scriptures (074) 42
(9) One's Success (075) 42
(10) There are Differences (076) 42
(11) Human Method (077) 43
(12) People Management (078) 43
(13) Man Doing Things (079) 44
(14) Human ability (080) 44
(15) With Sufficient Ability (081) 45
(16) Comparing Ability (082) 45
(17) All Kinds of Things (083) 45
(18) Frequent Comparison (084) 46
(19) Encounter Things (085) 46
(20) Take into Account the Big Picture (086) 47
(21) In Leadership (087) 47
(22) Rely on Yourself (088) 48
(23) For the Beginner's Mind (089) 48
(24) Fighting for the Honor (090) 49
(25) Some people (091) 49
(26) I Hate You (092) 50
(27) Heaven is Without Desire (093) 50
(28) Power is the Strength (094) 50
(29) Good Talent (095) 51
(30) Running Owards Unity (096) 51
(31) Buy, Lease, Borrow (097) 52

(32) The Mass Psychology (098) ……………………………… 52
(33) A Thousand Mile Journey (099) ……………………… 53
(34) Good Reputation (100) ……………………………………… 53
(35) For the Sake of Getting (101) ……………………… 54
(36) Two Roads (102) …………………………………………… 54
(37) Man, Food and Clothes (103) ……………………… 54
(38) A River (104) ………………………………………………… 55
(39) One Palm (105) ……………………………………………… 55
(40) Can I Do It (106) ………………………………………… 56
(41) Enjoying Labor (107) ……………………………………… 56
(42) Supply (108) …………………………………………………… 57
(43) Small Calculations (109) ……………………………… 57
(44) All Things Prosper (110) ……………………………… 58

Chapter 5

(1) One Person (111) …………………………………………… 60
(2) Three Goals (112) …………………………………………… 60
(3) Planning for the World (113) ………………………… 61
(4) How to Walk (114) ………………………………………… 61
(5) Want to Become Famous (115) ……………………… 62
(6) Have Faith (116) ……………………………………………… 62
(7) Multipolarization (117) …………………………………… 62
(8) Have Good Steel (118) …………………………………… 63
(9) Good Society (119) ………………………………………… 63
(10) Core Concept (120) ……………………………………… 64
(11) What to Think About (121) ………………………… 64
(12) Passing on from Generation to Generation (122) … 64
(13) Three Hundred Thousand (123) …………………… 65

第 一 章

（1）天地人（001）……………………………………………… 68
（2）你我它（002）……………………………………………… 68
（3）昨今明（003）……………………………………………… 69
（4）吃穿住（004）……………………………………………… 70
（5）安康福（005）……………………………………………… 71
（6）真正创（006）……………………………………………… 72
（7）假歪费（007）……………………………………………… 73
（8）危病亡（008）……………………………………………… 74

（9）数千年（009） …………………………………………… 75
（10）汉字创（010） …………………………………………… 76
（11）东方亮（011） …………………………………………… 77

第 二 章

（1）一二三（012） …………………………………………… 80
（2）出于蓝（013） …………………………………………… 81
（3）辩证律（014） …………………………………………… 82
（4）物三端（015） …………………………………………… 83
（5）先观察（016） …………………………………………… 84
（6）知其然（017） …………………………………………… 85
（7）时连续（018） …………………………………………… 86
（8）间接换（019） …………………………………………… 87
（9）温水物（020） …………………………………………… 88
（10）世界观（021） …………………………………………… 89
（11）动生换（022） …………………………………………… 90
（12）人遗传（023） …………………………………………… 91
（13）人自己（024） …………………………………………… 92
（14）私与公（025） …………………………………………… 93
（15）施仁政（026） …………………………………………… 94
（16）万物生（027） …………………………………………… 95
（17）万事物（028） …………………………………………… 96
（18）创系统（029） …………………………………………… 97
（19）留山水（030） …………………………………………… 98
（20）留智能（031） …………………………………………… 99
（21）想得到（032） …………………………………………… 100
（22）从从从（033） …………………………………………… 101

第 三 章

（1）金木水（034） …………………………………………… 104
（2）不吃穿（035） …………………………………………… 105
（3）什么事（036） …………………………………………… 106
（4）越前山（037） …………………………………………… 107
（5）悠悠地（038） …………………………………………… 108
（6）从一起（039） …………………………………………… 109
（7）糖尿患（040） …………………………………………… 110
（8）太大意（041） …………………………………………… 111
（9）身体差（042） …………………………………………… 112

（10）临危机（043）..113
（11）墙头草（044）..114
（12）临深溪（045）..115
（13）哪里来（046）..116
（14）好教育（047）..117
（15）古英雄（048）..118
（16）行千里（049）..119
（17）淡泊志（050）..120
（18）人客气（051）..121
（19）你有情（052）..122
（20）天下熙（053）..123
（21）人精神（054）..124
（22）有活力（055）..125
（23）粮油菜（056）..126
（24）养身体（057）..127
（25）关关鸠（058）..128
（26）君子交（059）..129
（27）亲兄弟（060）..130
（28）明知道（061）..131
（29）南辕辙（062）..132
（30）回头望（063）..133
（31）无心柳（064）..134
（32）我家乡（065）..135
（33）互联网（066）..136

第 四 章

（1）创善美（067）..138
（2）大学道（068）..139
（3）定时向（069）..140
（4）多和少（070）..141
（5）丛林中（071）..142
（6）熊掌鱼（072）..143
（7）物基础（073）..144
（8）天经义（074）..145
（9）成萧何（075）..146
（10）有差异（076）..147
（11）人方法（077）..148
（12）人管理（078）..149
（13）人做事（079）..150

条目	页码
（14）人能力（080）	151
（15）有足能（081）	152
（16）比能力（082）	153
（17）各种事（083）	154
（18）常对比（084）	155
（19）遇事情（085）	156
（20）顾大局（086）	157
（21）在领导（087）	158
（22）靠自己（088）	159
（23）为初心（089）	160
（24）争口气（090）	161
（25）有的人（091）	162
（26）我恨你（092）	163
（27）天无欲（093）	164
（28）权是力（094）	165
（29）好人才（095）	166
（30）奔统一（096）	167
（31）买租借（097）	168
（32）众心理（098）	169
（33）千里行（099）	170
（34）好信誉（100）	171
（35）为得到（101）	172
（36）路两条（102）	173
（37）人吃穿（103）	174
（38）一条河（104）	175
（39）一只掌（105）	176
（40）可不可（106）	177
（41）爱劳动（107）	178
（42）供供供（108）	179
（43）小九九（109）	180
（44）万事兴（110）	181

第 五 章

条目	页码
（1）一个人（111）	184
（2）三目标（112）	185
（3）谋万世（113）	186
（4）怎么走（114）	187
（5）想成名（115）	188
（6）有信仰（116）	189

（7）多极化（117） ……………………………………………… 190

（8）有好钢（118） ……………………………………………… 191

（9）好社会（119） ……………………………………………… 192

（10）核心观（120） …………………………………………… 193

（11）想什么（121） …………………………………………… 194

（12）万代传（122） …………………………………………… 195

（13）三百千（123） …………………………………………… 196

Chapter 1

(1) Heaven, Earth, and Man (001)

Heaven is empty, and it embraces all things in its entirety, allowing all things to operate in it. Earth, the rock and soil, is the foundation of all things; and by the cooperation of heaven and earth, all things come into being. Man is the gem of it, the soul of the universe; what kind of man is the deity who guards theuniverse?

(2) You, I, and It (002)

You, I, and he form a system; constrained by each other, balanced and stable. I am myself; you are the opposite; he is the third party, and we are to exchange in harmony. It is the broadest. It is the most numerous. There is someone outside of man, and there is heaven outside of heaven!

(3) Yesterday, Today, and Tomorrow (003)

Yesterday was changed for today, and it's gone; never to return, only to reminisce. Today will be changed for tomorrow, and it is right in front of you; if you don't cherish it and lose it, it will be too late to regret it. Tomorrow has not yet come. Where is it? We cannot get in, only to aspire! Yesterday, today, and tomorrow are two-way cycles; it comes from ancient times to recent times and the present!

(4) Food, Clothing, and Shelter (004)

To eat is as important as heaven and earth; it is energy and power. To wear is for protection, warmth, for beauty, for dignity. To dwell is to rest, that issleeping; there will be a good today with good sleep. To walk is to go, to move; true and proper action is bound to succeed! To be able is a purposeful power; it has to resort to methods and rely on exchanges to achieve its goals!

(5) Safety, Health, and Fortune (005)

Safety is to be safe, making decisions by oneself; often serious, no accidents. Health is to be healthy, mainly by parental inheritance; one's wellness is the capital of doing things. Fortune is about safety and health, and you feel comfortable and enjoyable; with happiness, be positive. Joy is the release of feelings and desires after getting and losing; Be kind and get happy. It is the ideal thing! Longevity is life span, and there are short and long;the more devotion, the longer life is!

(6) True Creation (006)

Truth is objectivity and law; we should follow nature and never stop. To be right is to be in the middle position, not to be crooked or biased; it is difficult to succeed in doing anything without objectivity and justice. Creation is the exchange, a kind of gain. It is about giving less and getting more. Goodness is to give love to others, a kind of devotion; after truly creating, one has to give out in the end. Beauty is goodness, a good feeling, like the sun, moon, and stars that light up the earth! Food and lust are the two natures of man; what is to be done to enhance them and reach a higher state?

(7) Fake Crooked Fee (007)

Fake is deceitful, that is, none; hypocritical people will not be submissive. Crooked is immoderate, deviating from the center; often distorted, it isdifficult to be just and balanced. A fee is to lose, an excessive consumption. One has to consume correctly, not waste. Evil is wickedness, a kind of harm; Harm others, one is bound to be harmed. Ugly is unsightly, a bad feeling; be brave enough to change so ugliness can change to be beauty!

(8) Danger, Sickness, and Death (008)

The danger is about the crisis, which starts to change in the wrong direction; to cure the disease before it takes place, to prevent it before it happens. Sickness is the disease, out of balance development. It can be reversed with reasonable action. Misfortune is a mishap, which has come; know the mistake, and start again from scratch! Suffering is misery, which is felt every day; to get the truth from it and dedicate to society. To die is to perish and become a cloud of smoke; ask Jesus in heaven, what age is it?

(9) Thousands of Years (009)

In thousands of years, the essence that mankind has gotten is materialism and dialectics. To be generous with virtue and self-improving. The first person who discovered dialectics was Fuxi. To rule by righteousness and use the military by wonder. The sacred text of dialectics is the Tao Te Ching. In the Art of War, with thirteen chapters, the use of dialectics has reached an apogee. The Tao is explicable, but not in general!A name is explainable,but not a general one!The Way of Heaven is to benefit all things without harm!The Way of Man is, to do something without striving for fame and profit!

(10) The Creation of Chinese Characters (010)

Chinese characters created, there comes the light of civilization. It is inclusive and open, spread to all directions. It helps to record things, aids in thinking, helps science and philosophy, helps to create correctly. The language has the same sound, and the characters have the same pattern; unified and convenient, moving forward and upward. Many Chinese literature are renowned; taste them finely, as if you were in the scene. A piece of ice heart is in the jade pot; the heart has a spiritual connection. A thousand pieces of gold are scattered but come back; I was born to have the talent to be useful!Liu Yuxi wrote "The Inscriptions of the Ugly Room"; Zhou Dunyi wrote "The Love of Lotus" to tell the affection of the lotus. The Book of Yueyanglou says, "The first day is the worry, the next day is joy"; "Drunken Master's Pavilion," Drunken Master's intention is not wine. The Six Towers of Jiang Shang, the Book of Scripture of Confucianism; Xunzi's Persuasion, The Technique of Mozi. The Joyful Rain of Spring Night, The Climbing of the Stork's Tower; The Leaving of the Grass on the Plain, May People last long!

(11) The East is Bright (011)

The East is bright, and the sun is coming out. As they spread virtue, all things are reviving. Chinese culture is profound; the Chinese language and writing are innovative. It is convenient to group and divide, easy to know the meaning; it is the first good tool. Concise and practical, easy to pass on. Eastern civilization, rising. Due to the complicated long and bland, it is difficult to circulate; Western civilization gradually lost. Who advanced set the standard; the higher the efficiency, the more attractive.

One Two Three

High technology, great strength, the good humanities will lead to unification. East and West, to be unified, rely on China, rely on the Chinese language. When China prospers, the world will rise; the global village will become a civilized place. Spoons are in the West; chopsticks are in the East; young and old use spoons, chopsticks are flourishing in middle age!

Chapter 2

(1) One, Two, Three (012)

One step, two steps, three steps, and you can move gold bricks; from three steps to two steps, then one step. It is smaller step by step. The individual obeys the public, that is, democracy; the public obeys individual management, that is one person is the master. Everyone tastes one sip, two sips, and three sips; from many sips to one sip, individuals enjoy. The stars shine from one star to many stars; from many stars to one day, the sun shines. The crowd is overwhelming from one son to many sons; from many sons to one son, only no more and no less is the most beautiful and sound!

(2) Derived from Blue (013)

Green comes out from blue is better than blue; one, two, three, cycle in both directions in the system. One becomes two; two becomes three; three produces everything, and then it changes in the opposite direction, less and less. The first is a state with solid, liquid, and gas; the second is property, feminine, masculine, and neutral. The third is primary and secondary, and there are three kinds of primary and secondary and secondary; the fourth is gradual, such as uniform acceleration The fifth is order, from grandfather to father to oneself; the sixth is the method, with a three-step approach. The seventh is the structure, and the family includes husband, wife, and children; the eighth is the function. There are three kinds of superior and secondary. The ninth is the system. The stellar system includes stars, planets, and satellites; the tenth is the cycle, sometimes thirty years.

(3) Dialectical Laws (014)

There are three dialectical exchange laws; understand the reasoning behind them, and the axiom is simple. An object is difficult to move; the exchange of multiple objects becomes the thing. The result is obtained by exchanging two objects: one of three results is greater than, less than and equal to one of the three results. They are equal in absolute value, and the sum of the two results is equal to zero. The volume is generally the smallest of the two sides and is the product of the exchange coefficient and the amount of participation. The amount of aggregation and dispersion of an object is equal to the product of the degree of exchange and time; the quantity is certain, and the degree is inversely proportional to time. The big universe, the small heaven, and earth; it all boils down toand one.

(4) The Three Ends of the Object (015)

There are two symmetrical ends in the three ends of the object. A good mid-range adjustment warms the heart. The object has three states, three properties; conditions change. A state, a performance; three states performance, generally only one exists. There is particularity with each object. There is a length with a feet. In universality, a feet is smaller than a yard. Opposites attract, same sexes exclude; the two sexes need each other and are difficult to separate. The structure of an object determines the performance; the form of a triangle is the most stable. The elements that make up a system need at least three; less than three is difficult to circulate. Stone, scissors, cloth make up the cycle;

one loop constrains the other and moves in one direction. Each link is critical; the most damning, the weak and transitional link!

(5) Observe First (016)

Observe first, then think; accumulate materials first, then classify. Comprehensive analysis: Look for the law; keep the law, and you are well and do not comply with the peril. There are three kinds of reasoning analogy, induction, and deduction; the law of cause and effect is easiest. The cause produces the effect, and the effect produces a new cause; the cycle of the law of causality leads to cyclical changes. Good deeds come back to help you, and bad deeds come back to haunt you; good and evil will have their karmic retribution when their time comes. Individuals make up the whole, and the whole is dispersed into individuals; when it is slow, the time is long; when it is fast, the time is short. To have a short time, you need to be fast; take your time to exist for a long time. Own slow or fast, feel other on fast or slow; own normal and stable, feel no change. One, two, three, three, two, one; four, five, six, seven, eight, nine. Things develop like waves; integrate at the bottom, then flourish!

(6) Knowing that This Is the Way It Is (017)

Knowing this, knowing why this is so, holding up one to the other, all things are connected. When it is pure, it is true; when it is dry, it is pure; when it is in the middle, it is right; when there is an opportunity, it moves. The person who unties the bell is sometimes the one who tries it; to stop the boil, one should first draw away the fire of the fire. If stability is required, the center of gravity needs to be below. Humility gets benefits, and complacency invites losses. To seek peace before seeking victory; to retreat before charging. The whole body is affected by one hair; the entire process must be serious. Cast a stone and think twice;

throw a brick, lift your clothes, take the collar first. Take one step, see many steps; use good external objects, pave the way in advance. Car in front, rut behind; feel the stone to cross the river! When the situation is confused, the onlooker is clear; partial hearing is dark, both listening is clear!

(7) Continuous Time (018)

Time is the continued existence of the object, and space is the extensive existence of the object; when the two are combined, the opportunity of the object comes into existence. There is simultaneity and co-location; no two chances are the same due to the change of space-time. The larger the object, the smaller the chance; the object's volume is inversely proportional to the opportunity. There are various opportunities for objects: good ones are cooperation; bad ones are war resistance. Lack and surplus are the prerequisites for constituting opportunities; the space of time in which the exchange takes place is the opportunity. Two objects can complement each other; the conditions for cooperation are fulfilled. Good exchange factor, good time-space; supply and demand exchange, all things flourish. To find the time, first, find the shortage; to satisfy the deficit, create the opportunity. The author of the poem "The Little Pond" is Yang Wanli; that dragonfly in the poem is very good at grasping the timing!

(8) Indirect Exchange (019)

Any exchange is an indirect exchange; it requires the help of intermediaries to be realized. There is nothing special about capable people; they are just good at utilizing the help of external objects. A workman must first sharpen his tools if he is to do his work well; rely on good talent to create number one. Stand high to look far; rely on the help of good external objects to develop. Suitable external objects are like wings; exchange them properly and let you soar. To select external objects, they must be up to standard; this includes high performance and low consumption. Selection of talent: the body must be fit; virtuous, capable, beautiful, and good at speech!

(9) Temperature, Water, and Substances (020)

With the proper mix of temperature, water, and material, the grass and trees will be produced; animals will appear with the exchange of grass and trees with water. Animals have evolved for billions of years. After man appeared, he slowly came to the top! Plants are kind and are animals' skies, making oxygen, food, shelter, and clothing. Animals are simple and naive; they do not change their clothes and do not dress up. Man is the most precious. Man is the most troublesome. Between life and death, things happen one after another. The many plants, like parents; without them, who would feed us? The many animals, like brothers and sisters; without them, who would keep us company? All matters, all creatures, have life; cherish more and seek to live together! From matter to plants to animals, man is the highest peak; when man reaches the top, he runs down and finally returns to the starting point!

(10) Worldview (021)

Worldview is the human point of view; methodology is how to exchange. Materialism speaks of objectivity; dialectics is used to guide practice. Matter, energy and information, all three are combined into one; matter, information is the appearance, energy is the soul. When matter is exchanged with energy, information appears; when objects are exchanged with objects, everything changes. If there are colored clouds in the morning, it may rain, so don't go out; if there are red clouds in the evening, it may be very hot tomorrow. If the swallow flies low and the snake

Chapter 2

slithers, heavy rain will come soon. Think of a way, take a sip of water; wash your hands well, it all depends on the control of your mouth. After the oil boils, dry it; then fry the dishes, less pollution, and the dishes smell good. After eating, pour some boiling water in the bowl; brush the bowl first, then rinse your mouth. The stomach aches, do not rush; untie the big hand, exhaust gas, maybe it will be fine!

(11) Motion Produces Exchange (022)

Movement produces exchange, and exchange produces quantitative change; at a right time, qualitative change will occur. To smooth the transition and prevent drastic changes; it is necessary to rely on reforms and adjust the quantitative changes. After getting equilibrium, the dynamic cycle begins; at a certain point, the quantitative and qualitative changes will begin again. Know the direction, you know the development trend; the general trend, understand the general. You can judge today's high and low by yesterday's high and low; you can predict correctly to know the real situation of the future. What is inevitable, be prepared in advance; what is possible, be prepared in many ways. It is important to prevent fire and thieves from stealing; to prevent the unexpected and being flooded. To be perfect, plan ahead; to do things ahead of time, where there is precaution, there is no danger! Ants shake the tree, it is ridiculous and over-confident; when the dike is destroyed by ants, how does it feel?

(12) Human Heredity (023)

Human heredity determines how good or bad a person's body is; the degree of metabolism of the body determines the amount of vitality. The vitality of a person determines the interests and hobbies of a person, the character, and the ability and goals. One's ability defines one's life; it determines the realm, life, career and the love relationship. After seeing and hearing, one knows;

after thinking, one makes a decision; by the body to walk, by the mind to feel. After knowing the truth, you determine the right path; after creating and giving, you feel good. Washington, the first president of the United States; truly wise and everlasting. Jiang Zhongzheng, who is also known as Kai-shek; telling lies, doing crooked things, leaving a thousand years of infamy. When the bird of prey is gone, the bow and arrow are useless; to know the right in and out, to be able to start well and end well!

(13) A Man Itself (024)

Man itself is the most important; without the self, it is all over for a man. What a man itself possesses, it is the most reliable; without privately owned, the man and his will run away. One has to be oneself first, then the periphery!To be privately owned first, and then talk about things like high-end public ownership! Throw yourself away, subservient to foreigners, helping others count the profit, which has been trapped. The enemy's friend, the enemy's enemy; in the end, whether it is a friend or a foe, it should be analyzed correctly. There is always yourself!There are eternal interests!There is no eternal friend!There is no eternal enemy! To love yourself, love each other; to love the third party, and grow together. All flowers will continuously bloom with a heart like a sea; create and give objectively and fairly, and goodwill come!

(14) Private and Public (025)

The private and the public are concerned with the individual and the whole; they transform each other and interact with each other. The private is the individual who needs possessions, freedom and equality. The public is the family, the group, the political party, the government and the state; the public is public power, supervision and management. The public is formed to better the private; to help protect the personal is the essential role of the public. If the public does not love the private, what is

Chapter 2

the use of the public? If the private does not love the public, the family and the country will be broken and drifting. If you want to enrich the country, you must first enhance the people!If you want to strengthen your country, you must first strengthen your army! When the private loves the public, it starts with me!When the public is perfect, that will benefit me! Turning private ownership into public ownership relies on justice and kindness!Riding the public into private depends on the fair exchange!

(15)Administering Benevolent Rule(026)

To administer benevolent rule is like the spring breeze; everything grows and goes smoothly. When tyranny is practised, it is like the cold winter; everything withers and difficulties abounds. Emperor Wen and Emperor Jing of the Han Dynasty, and Li Shimin of the Tang Dynasty; because of benevolent rule, there was unprecedented prosperity. Zhao Gao of the Qin Dynasty, Yang Guang of the Sui Dynasty; they died in the twinkling of an eye because of tyranny. Relying on punishment to achieve the purpose is unable to accomplish anything but liable to spoil everything. Ask the public, then determine the moral law; enforce it justly, and all will be happy. If there is a disagreement and a dissenting voice, the big trend has been formed. The big trend must be seen; to set early layout, steady compliance. To have more competition, less monopoly!Automation, is the most natural!

(16) All Things Grow (027)

All things grow, depending on heaven and earth; depending on the sun and moon, depending on the laws of nature. To follow the natural phenomena, follow the laws of nature, get true, and get a good rest. To hunt by deforestation, to fish by exhaustion; to be difficult to restore to the original state, to the detriment of others and oneself. For immediate benefit, the mountains are turned into flat land; the weather becomes arid, and sand and dust rise in all directions. The beautiful Yao Mountain has become a thing of the past; it has turned into a bottomless pit, and no one cares! The annual loss is difficult to calculate; local people rely on the sale of instant noodles to maintain their livelihood. Don't lose it, don't obscure it; landscape and trees are so pleasant for us! Good nature, like the Chinese language; colorful and enchanting!

(17) All things (028)

All things are tools, exchanging and using each other to go ahead. All things in the universe are different from each other according to the laws, operating in the system. There is metabolism, photosynthesis; there is nuclear fusion, oxidation reactions. Matter, energy and information make up the world; science, philosophy and literature make up studies. The two sides of the opposition, both contradictory and exchange; from opposition, resistance, to battle and negotiation. With more, they separate; with less, they gather; the best time is the middle! With a beginning, there is an end; the best is the process! The whole is absolute, and the individual is relative; the whole is unified, the individual is beautiful!

(18) Creation of the system (029)

Created the system methodology; Sun Wu of Wu State in the Spring and Autumn Period was the first man to do so. From the strategy of war to the methodology of war, "Sun Tzu's Art of War" had done with a systematic discussion. Determine the goal and make people yield; with the help of external objects, the Tao and the Law, the time and the place of heaven, etc. Know yourself and your enemy, and value yourself; in the temple, plan wisely. Take a step-by-step approach and attack one by one; improvise and ignore the king's orders. Grasp the timing, avoid the reality, surrender the soldiers, keep them if they are good, and finally do

Chapter 2

an excellent job in the aftermath. Knowing yourself is hard; acting correctly is hard; devotion is the hardest after actual creation! Knowing each other is difficult; reasonable exchange is difficult; becoming a soulmate is the most difficult! Where could be the difficulty for those who have a remarkable ability? To govern a big country is as easy as cooking a small meal!

(19) Leave the Landscape (030)

　　Leave the landscape, and the plants are beautiful; animals and people can consume. Reasonable consumption to meet needs; proper production, the system is intact. Consumption is giving, consumption is getting; consumption is converting, consumption is the goal. Objects are divided into three categories, industries are divided into four categories; in the end, they become consumption. The first is matter, the second is energy, and the third is information, three kinds in total. The first industry is industry, the second industry is transportation, the third is commerce, and the fourth is management. Processing, transportation, sales, consumption, recycling and reproduction; the need for intelligent management and circular development!

(20) Leave Intelligence (031)

　　Leave intellectual ability, and it would be everlasting; no after-effects, feeling relaxed. Foolish humans can't be too clever!Leave nothing for posterity, leaving after-effects! Objects of glass, shattered by people; hurting people and other things, whose sin is it? Plastic objects are thrown everywhere; the Pacific Ocean becomes unpeaceful. Some plants die, some animals die; it is difficult to secure the life of people. Artificial items, although convenient, some are difficult to decompose and pile up. No recycling, no reproduction; no more recycling will cause disaster. To develop well, we must recycle well; we must pay attention to recycling and reproduction. With such an item, it must be able to decompose it; not environmentally friendly and prohibited from circulation and production!

(21) Wishing to Get (032)

There is no ground for blame if you are so keen to obtain it; as long as you do not violate morality and law is acceptable. To gain is to lose; lose is to gain; to gain and to lose is fair, a balanced mind. Who gives, who gets; and who gets, who will get a guarantee! Who did wrong, who will redeem!Be courageous to undertake and will not regret! Those who sell plastic items should recycle the old plastic; those who sell items should recycle the outer packaging of the items. When there is garbage, it must be sorted; recycling, endless good. Stand in the middle, take a thorough account of the front and back; waste into the pit, toilet paper into the basket. Not to be mandatory, it is the truest; to see the actual situation, just go to the public toilet!

(22) Starting From (033)

From a point to a line, to the whole surface, there is a change in its nature with the change of quantity. From the gradual accumulation of soil to become a mountain of soil, the high end comes above the foundation below. From the internal situation to the external form, with a good internal structure, there comes excellent external performance. From a person to a system, there must be healthy competition to develop. From an individual point of view to the actual situation, follow the law, and develop. From a unique phenomenon to a universal law, be objective and fair first, and then create devotion. From the tribe to the union to the homeland nation; from the party-state to reach the republic afterward!

(1) Gold, Wood and Water (034)

Gold is getting more and more worthless like seawater; gold is getting less and less; what is rare is precious. It is as good as today from fewer trees to more trees; no more living trees can be seen, from more trees to deadwood. With more and more water, there will be fish jumping; plants and animals will leave and fly away with less and less water. Blaze burns from small fire to big fire; from big fire to small fire, only small fire remains. The soil becomes a mountain, the wind and rain float; the mountain becomes soil, there will be a sandstorm!

(2) No Food and Clothing (035)

How can you live and walk if you don't eat and wear? How can we have energy if we don't live and work? Without energy, how can we be well? Without well-being, how can we be blessed? Without bliss, how can we live longer? Without longevity, how can we be faithful? How can we create goodness if we are not faithful? Without virtue, how can we be beautiful? Learn to get genuine, think to get right; take action and get creation, with creation to get compassion, compassion to get kindness, and kindness to get goodness! First the hardware, then the software; synthesize the positive power to create goodness!

Chapter 3

(3) What's the Thing (036)

What are the things that we can do? What are the words that we can say? What is good for others and yourself can be said and done! Those that harm others and oneself cannot be said or done! There are rules for the operation of all things; people must obey the law and morality. A true creation of goodness and beauty is morality, the soul of the law; in exchange, gain and loss are to be balanced without contradiction. The morality of man is divided into three types; from low to medium to high, step by step to be nobler. For good morality, one must consciously abide by it; when someone violates it, it relies on everyone to speak up to stop it. A good law must be objective and fair. Whoever crosses it must be severely punished! All abide by morality, the law is not in use; everything is good in its place, and everyone is noble. If I'm wrong, say, "I'm sorry! " "I am to forgive you, it's okay! "If you help me, I say, "Thank you! We help each other, you're welcome! "

(4) Crossing the Mountain In Front(037)

Cross the mountain in front of you to reach the world behind it; filial piety is one of the virtues to be held above all else and having no offspring is the worst one of the ways being unfilial to our parents. It is the truth of the three principles that a monarch governs his ministers, a father governs his sons, and a husband governs his wife. Guan Zhong of Qi established the four dimensions: integrity, shame and etiquette. Confucius, Mencius and Dong Zhongshu established the five constants: benevolence, righteousness, propriety, wisdom and faith. Sun Wu of Wu, established the five things: the Way of Heaven and Earth and the Law of Generalship. The five conditions of a good commander are: wisdom, faith, benevolence, courage and severity. In the old society, the five virtues were taught: gentle, kind, respectful and frugal. To repay virtue with virtue, and to repay grievances with rectitude; those who violate me, though far away, must be punished!

(5) A Life of Ease (038)

A land of ease, a sky of leisure; respecting all things, man is the most splendid. As we sow, so shall we reap; we get what we plant. With good management, you get a good harvest. The first is before birth, relying on parents to bear; before conception, one must be safe and healthy. The second is the family and school as the underlying factor behind. One needs a good family, a beautiful school. The third is to enter society. We all have to monitor together; a good life depends on oneself to achieve. First of all, we should eat and dress reasonably and then live and act appropriately; first, we should have the ability to take care of ourselves and stand on our own. The biggest enemy is yourself; manage yourself well, and may everything you do come your way. To succeed, first, you have to design; with the help of external objects, rely on ability. A man should deliver a service of collaborative process wholeheartedly from the beginning to the end; this is the state's strategy that should be vigorously pursued!

(6) Starting from Together (039)

I want to be well so badly, yet it cannot happen; the disease inherited from my parents adds to my worries. Who will determine my fate? It is the parents who decide the victory or defeat! One's parents, inadvertently; their children, have the likelihood of suffering for a lifetime. It all involves genetics, nutrition, education, and other growth factors. The fate of their children is in the hands of their parents!Before conceiving, you need to test if the seeds are good! Without a good seed, please don't plant it blindly!Without the ability, don't give birth! The actual starting line is here!This is the most important

Chapter 3

thing, and this is the most urgent thing that needs to be done! The country needs to set up a fertility fund and set up fertility health hospitals!For the sake of future generations, be selfless! Individuals, families and nations, pay attention as soon as possible!For the sake of two and three, start with one!

(7) Diabetic Patients (040)

People with diabetes are the most suffering and hardest!The hardship is like hell on earth. It's so tough to talk! Look at the outside, and it is very sound; who knows the inside? It is too unfortunate. The powerlessness of the inner mind, interests and hobbies are bland; the powerlessness of the body, which can only listen and see but cannot do. The heart is bleak; the road is long; who would know that? And who will care? This charity, that charity; why not lean forward to help a little? Thoughts remain thoughts, and reality remains reality; one's suffering is felt only by oneself. There is no way out of the mountain; where is the light at the end of the tunnel?

(8) Too Much Carelessness (041)

When I was young, I was too careless; in order to earn money, I harmed my body. In middle age, the disease is haunted; there is nowhere to find a good feeling. People have been sick for a long time, carelessly seek medical help; take too much medicine, and hurt their vitality. One move goes wrong, and the subsequent moves turn wrong, too; nowadays, it is challenging to help oneself. Human suffering is also a kind of blessing!Suffering resources are to be adequately interpreted! Human life, for the sake of feeling and ideal; as long as people live, there is hope to achieve their wishes! Start from now, start from yourself!Recuperate and prepare to rise again! Before dawn, the night is bleak; amid helplessness, hoping for having Sun Yang, the talent scout! The more you think it is hard, the longer you feel about the time; only in the midst of creation, you can see hope!

(9) **Poor Health** (042)

Poor health, fear of everything; what should be taken cannot be taken, what should be put away cannot be put away. Small vigor, big ideas; often fantasize, often depressed. The ability is small; thinking about the wrong things; it is discouraged when it comes to sight. Not as good as others, generating jealousy and hatred, not looking for their fault, and sometimes gloating. Why are we not as good as others? The root cause is our own factors! Why is it that you are not as good as others? Some of the reasons lie in the genetics of parents! Feelings in the head, the actual body, organ problems, and cells are the root cause. If a person is sick, it isn't easy to take care of oneself!If the country is sick, it isn't easy to establish dignity! To prevent and cure diseases, we must start from the root; people form nations, and nations are like individuals. To impart knowledge, first, impart morality!To cure poverty, first, cure disease!

(10) **In the Face of Crisis** (043)

In the face of crisis, in the depths of suffering, should we have done what we did in the past if we had known it? The past feeling is gone; things have not changed, but I have changed. The genes have changed, and the energy is scattered; I don't want to see such a world anymore. The earth has feelings, and the god has eyes to judge; being in the human world will make one most unwilling to leave! The decades of human life are in the blink of an eye; sooner or later, all have to go there. When one dies, the soul goes to heaven; the body turns to ash and returns to nature! Looking for the people before you, you need to go to the shrine; there is no tombstone, and the plants flourish. To build a shrine, return to the homeland, return to the roots, and return to heaven!

Chapter 3

Heaven on earth, how to go up? The pursuit of the true, perfect good creation! Family regulations need to be objective and fair; family prospers, and the world civilizes!

(11) Grass on the Wall (044)

The grass on the wall falls with the wind; nature will be good with a forest. Who would like to become grass when you can become a tree? Who wants to run on the ground when you can ride in a car? The survival of the fittest; without foundation, it is difficult to move up. You have a great ambition, but you can't afford to do it; no one cares, no one asks. Cry out to the heavens, but the heavens don't respond. Cry out to the earth, but the earth is impervious; it is difficult to shed tears, difficult to be touched. Human beings!Man, man!Who knows, my piece of suffering? First the world's worries, then the world's happiness, sounding into the ears, caring about everything! Pointing to the mountains and talking about heroes, I want to go home and grow vegetables for a living. The grass is by the river, looking up at the clouds; if I reach the top, I can see all the mountains! Who is the master of the world? It depends on the present day!Whoever can be true is the best!

(12) Facing a Deep Stream (045)

Only when you face a deep stream can you know that the earth is abundant; only when you climb a high mountain can you know that the sky is high. Without low, how can there be high? Without low tide, it is hard to have high tide! Since ancient times, there have been many trials and tribulations for males; there are fewer great men among fops. Often hate it when somebody fails to live up to your expectations; too dense planting produces less food harvest. Chicken feathers in exchange for garlic skin, the more you change it, the less you get; five horses in exchange for six sheep, the more you change it, the less strong it is. Pick up sesames and lose the watermelon; one often loses a lot due to trivial ones. Through the suffering, only then know how to cherish!Experiencing setbacks, and you will understand things! Gaining from failure is the most impressive!Paid for failure, it does not matter! Learn the history, grow from experience; do not listen to the older man's words, suffer losses in front of you. It is difficult to create the future without inheriting the past; it is difficult to accelerate forward without making the transition!

(13) Where Do I Come From (046)

Where do I come from? Where to go? Which roads to take? Who will accompany me on the route? You are born of your mother, so to go to heaven!The colorful road, the true creation of goodness and beauty! When a person is born, he is neutral; later on, good or bad, it depends on how to appreciate it. There is no lazy one next to the diligent one; if you are faithful, he will go on to create goodness. To teach by example is the most effective; the drizzle is like fine rain. One has to tell the facts and reason, talk about the mind and sense. The more you scold, the more you deviate from the right, difficult to defuse, rebellious mentality. The frequent actions become habits; habits become nature; nature is a trait that is very difficult to change! From the good or bad at the age of three, you can tell how good or bad one is when one grows up, and from the age of seven, you can tell how one will be for the rest of the life; essential education, is the most important!

(14) Good Education (047)

Good education, where is it? Many people are looking for it. Where are the swift horses? Where are the talents? Read "The Sayings of the Horse " and ask Han Yu. Eight hours, a working day; children's learning, how many hours would you say? From dawn to late at night; lack of lunch break, studying hard. Students who suffer are like slaves; overworked, uninterested. Words as small as rice work as high as a mountain; the spine becomes bent and becomes myopic. Being exhausted, who is going to mind it? Who will take the responsibility after it? A good education strengthens the body!Teach to behave and grow in capability! Music, chess, calligraphy, and painting; morality, intellectuality, and martial arts; how to learn without a curriculum? Education reform is the most urgent need; I hope there will be joint efforts from the entire community!

(15) Ancient Heroes (048)

Since ancient times, heroes have emerged from the youth; to become successful, train from childhood. Get up earlier, sleep earlier; what needs to be done, do it uninterruptedly. Who knows that every grain of food is hard work; need to save, need to be simple. Set your goals according to your interests; take the nearest available materials and advance step by step. At home, obey your parents!At school, listen to your teachers! Do your own thing, do it yourself; doors, windows, etc. , always think about turning them on and off. Exercise your ability to swat flies; What flies, what moves, what is still, hit a hundred times. When there is danger, call quickly; think of ways to escape! Be clean and neatly dressed; knock gently on the door and enter after getting permission. Say hello and indicate your intention; show more respect and express your gratitude!

(16) Traveling a Thousand Miles (049)

When a child travels a thousand miles, his mother worries; put your parents' affairs before yours! Outside the home, you need to be careful; do not get proud, be careful to help others. If you want to take advantage of a bargain, you will likely be cheated! Don't eat free meals; don't pick up money when you see it. Habour no ill intention against others, but never relax vigilance against evil-doers. Work with a righteous heart!There is nothing to be ashamed of in your heart, so not afraid of ghosts! Before crossing the road, stop for a while; pass quickly when the car is far away. Save at home, be rich on the road, and prepare enough food, drink, clothing, and money! Driving at night, encountering cars and people, and changing to the low beam is a kind of due diligence. If it's a good car, don't block the road; if it's a good person, don't block people's doors!

(17) The Spirit of Equanimity (050)

To be aloof and clear-headed, serene and far-reaching; to remove evil and do righteousness. Knowing honesty and shame, knowing etiquette; nothing is deceitful! If it's your own, fight for it; if it's someone else's, don't think about it. No harm, seek win-win; stop when appropriate, and act according to your ability. Exchange if it fits, leave if it doesn't; never push to ask, never ask for a stay. Take a step back and get some clarity on the situation. Some compromise brings peace of mind; suffering a loss is a blessing, give up to gain. People who lack virtue bully the kind and the weak; One should do self-defence and do boldly for what is righteous. The heart should be big. The power should be great. It is vital to be able to take up and also to let go!

(18) The Polite Manner (051)

When others are polite, please don't take them seriously; when you are polite, be genuine. Do not forget the goodness of others; do not mention your own goodness. Think of your faults, do not reveal the shortcomings of others; silence is golden, smile more and say less. Sickness comes from the mouth, and trouble comes from the mouth; strictly control the mouth, and be safe at all times of the year! To respect the privacy of others; do not speculate, do not spread. Don't get close to pornography, gambling and drugs; once you lose your footing, it will become a thousand years of regret!

Chapter 3

(19) You Have the Love (052)

You have genuine feeling; I have a friendship; doing things together will be easy. Often interact and grow in love over time; no more extended contact becomes strangers. Be more respectful and encouraging; do not complain, not discourage. Good friends depend on each other for a long time; trust each other and have no secrets. You help others, and others help you!Equivalent exchange is the objective truth!

(20) The Hustle and Bustle of the World (053)

The world is bustling, all for profit; the world is bustling, all for benefit. Spending money is easy and earning money is difficult; how can we make a long term living without being careful and steady? You go to manage your money, money will take care of you; more efforts, more gains. When you have eggs, put them in multiple baskets; when you have money, put them in multiple places. To go around more, to see more; after exploring more than one, you are to exchange decisively. Let you pre-pay, not to pay or pay less; these are to avoid, falling into the trap of others!

(21) The Human Spirit (054)

The human spirit factor, is very important; someone got to the hospital and the sickness had just been cured. Usually, the mood is very good; when something happens, it is troubled. Immediately gain or loss, the heart can not stand; this is the alarm bell is ringing, must know! If you have something in your heart and are unhappy, you must release it by talking, shouting and crying. Not through the mouth is also possible; please write it out with your pen. You can run, stretch your arms; you can also climb the mountain, look at the sea. Shed the load, strong body; good life, always belong to you. Not in its place, not seeking its politics; people retired, easy on the mind!

(22) **Having Vitality** (055)

 With vitality, one feels amazing; the right feeling is the purpose of life. Vitality determines feeling, and thoughts produce dreams; in sleep, one needs to pee; sometimes, one seeks the pit when one dreams. Action makes one feel good and most capable; thinking and dreaming will be better. We might have a poor sense of movement, but we can have good thoughts. We could be more relaxed in the dream with moderate physical condition. Just dreaming feels good; the body has gone down; thinking and moving are difficult to adapt. Even dreams are not good, and the body may already be sick; need to recuperate as soon as possible and do things slowly! Action, thoughts, and dreams need different vitality; sequentially, we must obey from big to small. Seeing is not as good as hearing; because hearing brings thought; seeing brings action. When you feel good, you have more confidence; no matter what you do, you are not afraid!

(23) **Food, Oil, and Vegetables** (056)

 Necessities are, in descending order, food, oil, vegetables, salt, eggs, and milk; the most thirst-quenching is warm plain water. We should eat more vegetables and fewer grains; we should eat less salt and preferably no sugar. Chew slowly, feel sweet; genetically healthy, vitality arises. Set the amount and time, follow the correct order; no added chemicals, vegetables nourish people. Eat less meat, no smoking, no alcohol; frequent meditation, frequent lunch breaks. Frequent changes, frequent conditioning, good health, balance of yin and yang. The multi-pronged approach is the right medicine; hot noodles with ginger can cure a cold. Living reasonably will be the best medicine; To cure disease, rely on sleep! The life cycle is twelve; the proper traditional Chinese medicine treatment is the best way to protect health!

Chapter 3

(24) Nourishing the Body (057)

To take care of the body, start from childhood; treat yourself well for the sake of safety and health. People's blood sugar determines people's vitality; normal and stable, is the most powerful! If one organ is hindering, multiple systems will be implicated. Weak parts should be protected; unifying the regulation relies on the brain. If the mouth, throat and eyes are dry; it means that there is a shortage of endocrine. Relax your body, close your eyes; breathe deeply, and slowly stretch your limbs. More saliva, tears out of the eyes; doing the fitness work can end it. After lying down, you can meditate adequately, shed tears, and have more happiness. Lie down like a bow, sit like a golden bell; stand like a green pine, walk like a fast wind! Chinese Tai Chi, Indian Yoga Gong; there is the same principle, different methods.

(25) Guan Guan Dove (058)

Guan!Guan!Cry the fish hawks, on sandbars in the river; a mild-mannered good girl, fine match for the gentleman. Vast grasslands, immense sky of clouds, there is a fair lady, across the water. A good temperament, pure, clean, spiritual; heavy makeup, has lost the real nature. A good man, great in ability; truly creating, protecting the country. Good woman, gentle, kind, beautiful; self-reliance and self-improvement without nagging. Man with double gene is easy to cease to be faithful; woman, with a single gene, is the most innocent. Your own children are the closest to you; do not move by the beauty of others' spouses. Like-mindedness, mutual concern; the longer the love, the deeper the friendship!

(26) Gentleman's Friendship (059)

A gentleman's friendship is as mild as water; do your best if there is something to do. The friendship of a villain does not taste like water; if something big happens, each one flees. Water the tree and water the roots; make friends with people; learn to be grateful to each other! Turnip is reaching the end and needs not to wash its mud; hungry and thirsty people tend not to be picky. When others face difficulties, we go to the rescue; others will not forget that in their lifetime. A horse's strength will be known by a long-distance travel, while a person's heart will be revealed by time.

(27) Dear Brothers (060)

Close brothers also need to clear accounts; confused accounts will cause harm to peace. Things should be clearly stated and understood beforehand; the correct process cannot be missing. Between relatives, it is best not to have deals on money; when it is not handled well, both parties will get upset. You treat him % good, yet with % bad; he may not count your good deed as one but will deeply remember your bad. In drawing a tiger, you show its skin, but not its bones; in knowing a man, you may know his face, but not his heart. Old cattle like to eat young grass; an older man likes to marry a young girl. There is a big difference between cows and grass; older men and girls are all humans, getting what they expect. Toads want to eat swan meat; there is hope if you create it. Liu Bang of Han Gaozu, Zhu Yuanzhang of Ming Dynasty; who would have thought that they could become emperors?

(28) Knowing Obviously (061)

I know apparently that it is wrong; why don't I correct it? Because it has been wrong for a long time and has become a habit, it feels unnatural if you change it again. It is easy to get on the boat but hard to get off; it is hard to return if you are not strong. It is easy to go down but hard to go up; it is difficult to create goodness if you are not objective and fair. Hanging a horse from a cliff, turning back is the way to shore; bear the pain for the benefit of the long term. Just as bitter medicine cures sickness, so unpalatable advice benefits conduct. Exotic stones can help to carve a native jade. An advice of others can serve to correct our faults. The monk from afar is good at reading scriptures - the foreign talent is valued higher than local talent!

(29)Going South in Wrong Direction(062)

Go south by driving the chariot north -act in a way that defeats one's purpose; when will it reach the state of Chu? The wolf and the lamb contradict themselves; The fox uses the tiger's power, with bitter incisiveness. Cover your ears and steal the bell, ccarve a mark on gunwale in moving boat where a sword was lost -ridiculous stupidity; The man who rather trusted his measurements than placing any confidence in his own feet when buying shoes -rigidly follows the rules. Guard the plant and wait for the rabbit, pull up the Seedlings to Help Them Grow; Lord Ye professed to love dragons, there is no hope. The farmer and the snake, Dong Guo and the wolf; a well-regulated mind, no longer reckless. The pony crosses the river, mend the fold after the sheep have been stolen- better late than never; the crow drinks water, never waits for help. Pan Gu created heaven and earth- the beginning of the world, Yugong moved the mountains- the determination to win victory and the courage to surmount every difficulty; the tortoise and the hare race, the tortoise relies on the long-lasting perseverance!

(30) Looking Back (063)

Looking back, my hometown; there are many interesting stories, according to the legend. The girl on the nun, the head activity; the nest of Gogongzhuang, breathing above. Xiao Xin village in the west, Guo Gu village in the east; because of carelessness, she married to Guo Gu village. In Zhanghua Fort, there is a Zangmi Temple; In Fortress City, there is an old man. What can't be smashed, my pot; what can't be drenched, my car. Dong Lv Zhuang, the spirit is not united; has not dug a well, two cast plays. The one who digs his own well is, the military examination graduate of the Sun family; Sun Laohe, specializing in maiden opera. Three black land, two white land, a cauliflower in the head. Liu family adopts a son, writing to send the evidence; clearly in the deception, it is difficult to justify! Say no, but send it to the house at night; the building on the farm, is the Ren family's!

(31) The Unintentionally Planted Willow (064)

A watched flower never blooms, but an untended willow grows. Man proposes, God disposes. Slap one's face until it is swollen in an effort to look imposing -do something beyond one's means in order to be impressive; gentility without ability is worse than plain beggary. Zhou Yu beat Huang Gai, and one is willing to fight, one is willing to take; who is the sad one in the human world? Sit in a well and look at the heaven-limited outlook, the ludicrous conceit of the king of Yelang - parochial arrogance; the king bids farewell to his concubine and dies at the end of the days. Fear of wolves in the front, fear of tigers in the back; after gaining and losing, do you realize? You wear out iron shoes in fruitless searching. A canal is formed when water comes; doubts will clear up when facts are known. There is no fish in the river, so you go to the town market to see; the bigger the woods, the more complete the birds. Mantis catching cicadas, the yellow bird in the back; create a dedication to the good, justice without worry!

(32) My Hometown (065)

My hometown, both arid and bleak; the good old days are in dreamland. Weather conditions go downhill; the good environment is shrinking. Either drought or drowning, cold or hot; where is the comfort? Trump, you, he, and I; Do not die to live! Nature is unbiased; more in less, reciprocal exchange. More water on the ground, flooding in the sky; the drier the ground, the drier the sky. Wind and rain, the system is sound; all segments, harmoniously connected. Fake crooked fee up, evil and ugly followed; truly created, good and beautiful followed!

(33) The Internet (066)

The Internet is the most beautiful and most tempting; it can go for good and bad things. Used well, it can create good and beauty; used badly, individuals and families may be ruined. Fiddle with cell phones, obsessed with games; stay up at night, not in the morning. Physical fatigue, depressed mood, delayed work, delayed study. In the future, make laws; restrict online loans and games. Control your cell phone usage, work and rest well; create and give rightly, and everyone likes you. Good faith, good goal; good with the phone, you can get to the goal in advance. Freedom to move relies on balance; the self-control to move relies on the real. Chinese culture and cell phone networks are the hope for the real creation of goodness and beauty!

Chapter 4

One Two Three

(1) The Creation of Infinite Beauty (067)

Without truth, how can reality exist? Without reality, how can there be Creation? Without Creation, how can there be perfection? Without Perfection, how can there be beauty? Without beauty, who do we sing praises to? Without anything, isn't it saddening? The infinite Creation follows the law of Truth. Man has a skewed perception of things, even though they have both palms. To be honest, this is something beyond challenge, how can we fulfil the contribution to the Creation of Fairness? It can be considered as the truth, but the Truth can also be deniable as well. Without facts, how can we ascertain that it is indeed the Truth? We often perceive deception as truth, and truth as deception, when our hearts are filled with wickedness, the world will be defeated by evil! Without rain clouds, it's impossible to have rainfall. It's only with Truth, that the Creation of Perfect Beauty can be possible!

(2) The Way of The Great Learning (068)

The way of The Great Learning is definitely wise; being friendly and approachable, is no short of doing good. Knowing when

Chapter 4

the stop creates stability, with stability comes peace of mind, with peace of mind, comes calmness, and with calmness, comes humility. There is a beginning and an end to things, and there is always a beginning and an end to things; if you know the order of things, you will be close to the Path of Truth. First, we will get rid of our selfish desires, then we will find the Truth; first, we will have sincerity, and then righteousness will follow. We must first cultivate our own spirit, followed by that of our families; then heal our country and hence bring forth everlasting peace to the world. The way of The Great Learning, the view of The Doctrine of the Mean; it's indeed the essence of the True Creation of Goodness and Beauty! What is the root? What is the end? Know the cause and effect, then think and do!

(3) Focus on Time and Direction (069)

To ascertain the time and direction, we need to be guided by Sun, the Northern Star facing Southwards. Man has ten fingers, by using the decimal system; the orbit of the moon and planet Earth determines their roundness and time. Those who can see it can have access to the Path of high morale, for those who don't see it, it will be chaotic. Although the county officials are large in numbers, they are no longer in charge now; although there is much water from afar, it does not help quench our thirst. We must accept compromises, and don't be headstrong about things. We can lose a little, but not too much. We must consider being fair, as it reflects our strength. To prove that it's true, evidence is needed. If there is no truth, indefinitely, the after effect will definitely be hard to handle!

(4) More or Less (070)

Whether it's "more" or "less", these two are our fundamental needs; the excess will be considered as Expenses, while less will be considered an Income. Without such needs, then there is no motivation for us to grow; without growth, there is no such need exists. Our needs and personal growth are just like "the chicken and egg" philosophy, where it is passed down from generation over generation. The same needs are bound to compete. By fulfilling mutual needs, it creates a win-win situation. Having the ability to decide on a particular matter, depends on our willpower. When there are mutual needs, it will create a well proportionate balance. A well-managed problem is dependent on our power to manage things well. We must think of how we could succeed, as it is with such power that there will be an equilibrium! Our thoughts and actions will have cause and effect; and ultimately our needs and personal growth, are very much dependent on how we think and what we do!

(5) In the Jungle (071)

The jungle is filled with the most barbaric animals, where the strong eat the weak, there is no sense of orderThe predators are "kings" of the jungle, and the preys are the weak; whoever is stronger, shall become hegemony. Comply in appearance but oppose in heart, a thief posing as judge, play the trick of thief crying 'Stop thief '". Such world is even darker than the kingdom of wolves. By virtue of falsehood, gain, sinfulness and wastefulness, I still think its very beautiful. It's his own wicked heart that had caused the disaster; whining about the moon is pure nonsense. Only by holding a highly respectable position, one can gain the most profit; one only knows how to sweet talk, but never does the right thing. Only this could make people anxious; in desperation, they left their homes and in search of other places to make a living. Even with Justice, creation and dedication are nothing; it is hard to be popular, and that is saddening! People betray their relatives and leave, in search of Goodness and Beauty; if they disobey, it will surely lead them towards self-destruction! The world is as black as a crow; become a swan and fly upward!

Chapter 4
(6) The Bear's Paw and the Fish (072)

Between a bear's paw and a fish, choose one, if you choose the bear's paw, then you should forego the fishLife, properties, and fame, comparing their rank of importance, we need to first secure our lives, followed by our private properties and fame. The philosophy of Liu, fighting to be the owner of the land; between these two, who is more stupid? True wisdom, with solid desire; how can we ensure there won't be any injury? We must learn how to adapt and find a solution, every road leads to Beijing! A town has its council, which the city must follow; changes can occur randomly, and our hearts should always be focused and upright. Even the strongest can suffer breakdown, and the weak can change; it is most beautiful to see the strongest and the weakest working synergistically together! What we don't need, might be something of a necessity to others; why would giving others be considered inappropriate?

(7) The Foundation of the Object (073)

Objects are the foundation, and people are the top-layer structure; objects determine people, and people use objects. People and resources need to remain in equilibrium with the right proportion; family planning is a great plan for thousands of years ahead! Having a reasonable amount of savings is a great thing, without savings, our livelihood would not be secured. The difference between incoming and outgoing determines how much is stored; it is necessary to properly diversify sources of income and reduce expenditures to create more wealth. What we should contribute must be no less than a cent!Whatever income we have, we must always keep it safe! We must think about creating wealth, and there are many ways to do so; prenatal and postnatal care, and always care for the plants! If you wish to eat, you can cook something at home; if you want to dress, it should be pure cotton. Having a clean stomach, with a pureness of heart, makes one feel good, and enhances longevity!

(8) The Meaning of the Scriptures (074)

According to the scriptures of Genesis, the moon orbits around the Earth, and the Earth orbits around the sunStanding on the ground, looking up at the sun and the moon; why does the moon appear incomplete? The rainforest filled the buildings with blowing winds, looking at the yellow pastures, we will know that autumn is near. We can't see clearly, and it's beyond comprehension; keeping a good distance, beautiful haze. The truth can sometimes be hidden; to seek knowledge, we need to listen and think. People needs, something new, something different, and something delicious!The more you repeat, the more disgusted you will feel! In this infinite world, there are thousands of species; peace and unity are what bring prosperity. The benevolent love the mountains, the wise loves the water; the high mountains are adored, absolutely beautiful indeed!

(9) One's Success (075)

The key to one's success is also one's undoing; he monopolizes, others can hardly live. If everyone, are too easygoing; collide with each other, it is bound to be chaotic. Beneficial to one side, but harm the other; there is a vicious circle to appear, how to manage? For their own sake, to take into account each other; control themselves, love multiple parties. More tolerance, more consultation; equality and give way to each other, the road is wide. Do it separately, the positive creation will be more; the inferior to give way, the superior to go up! Use what he needs, in exchange for what I need; rely on objective and fair, to undertake to ensure! All for one, one for all; meeting the wishes of the people, you will be embraced by the public!

Chapter 4

(10) There are Differences (076)

If there are differences, be different from the object; if the other party has a bottom line, do not transgress. Know the priority first, and then set the latter and first; follow the order and develop gradually. Hard within soft, straight in the middle; fast or slow and other methods to choose as needed. Reward and punishment should be strict and moderate, and they can't be lighter or heavier. Those who have morality and ability must undertake more responsibilities; items often used to be placed in the front position. To use the real, weigh the pros and cons; determine the present, and look to the future! To help it grow if the good outweighs the bad; to control its lifeline if the bad outweighs the good!

(11) Human Method (077)

The human method is science and technology; it is the sequence of doing things, plus the rationing of raw materials. It is better to teach a person the method of how to get the item than to give him the item; when you get the method, you create the ability. One-to-one exchange method; it is the most efficient and easiest. Healthy competition is a good method; you will be advanced with the competition. Weakening the opponent is a bad method; there will probably be no long-term benefit if you gain just in the near future. Helping the exchange party is a good way; more exchange, more benefit. The same words with different ways of saying them will produce different results. The same thing can come with a different approach; a good approach will produce good results. All kinds of things, like to be mild; gradually exchanged from slow to fast, more to gain! Bad and good methods are subject to comparison; there is no best, only better!

(12) People Management (078)

One Two Three

Human management is an ability; all things are easy when the ability is great. When the body is good, the feeling will be marvelous; when the physical and mental strength is vigorous, the confidence will be strong. With vitality, ideals will arise; then, look for goals and directions. After determining the goal and direction, you have to look for the way; then apply good methods to act. Power is the key after finding the object, exchange, and the four elements of ability. With the goal, you need to plan, design, and then follow a certain method to do. With the generation of ability, the step of commodity exchange and its value will certainly be realized!

(13) Man Doing Things (079)

One does things just like playing chess; one needs to observe more and analyze more. The right perspective, beautiful sight and sound; to understand clearly from many aspects. Listen to their words and observe their actions; if people are not correct, do not work with them. Know all kinds of things and have one proficiency; create special items that billions of people use. To do big things, you need to concentrate big forces; choose one, and back up several behind. To be successful, you need multiple systems; each link has close synergy. Put in the right position, each responsible for their own; the right exchange, common development. Always check, look for hidden dangers, eliminate them correctly, ensure peace! Always prepare, create opportunities; when the time comes, correctly create goodness and beauty!

(14) Human ability (080)

Human ability is the most important! Everything, rely on it! To recognize their actual situation, according to their own ability, determine the size of the dream. Ability is big; put in efforts to develop, open up the territory; ability is small, back off, do some

Chapter 4

simple things. Before you do something, think about it! After making it, what will be the result? If you have the ability, do it with all your might; otherwise, you will be scolded and hated for hurting people's hearts. If you don't have the conditions, don't do it; that's the real responsibility! When it's critical, you must be calm and steady; if you don't know how to do it, don't do it! To use the actual data, judge right after, and be decisive and brave! One step to the top, one step in place; do things to excess, sure to regret!

(15) With Sufficient Ability (081)

People with sufficient ability are often capricious, for good results are in their own hands. When people are rich, they like to be capricious; too much waste to be happy. Young people, sometimes capricious, slowly figure it all out after encountering setbacks. People with wisdom and ability, often hidden from the public; do big things, easy as pie. A bottle being not full, people with half a bottle shaking; like to show off, sometimes to get unwillingly dragged into something. The bigger the tree, the more it will attract the wind; the tree wants to stay still, but the wind does not stop. There are many reasons to figure out; change your own bad, learn to use others' good!

(16) Comparing Ability (082)

Comparing ability, not as strong as you; but comparing education, it's higher than you! Comparing the work efficiency, it is not as high as you; but comparing the relationship with the leader, it's better than you! Comparing the academic performance, it is not as good as you; but comparing the seniority, it is older than you! Without objectivity and fairness, one gets disappointed and escapes; create good beauty, no opportunity! To develop, we must reform; don't just talk and not do! Just say good things; it is not helpful; the key is to see how the action is! Be it a mule or a horse, come out to see it, then you will know; to use the truth to test!

(17) All Kinds of Things (083)

There are limits for doing all kinds of things; put the limits well, then you will be mature. Sometimes you know it, but do not say it out; end it at the right point and intentionally save face for others. Observe the real, do not do more than necessary; encounter unusual circumstances, deal in a special way! The most valuable thing about people is that they know their strengths and weaknesses; after comparison, they are aware of their little ability, thus, not to do it! With their own eggs, bumping other people's stones; that is not only unsightly but also unpleasant. The sticky cake is too sticky and too soft; it is difficult to get off if it sticks to you. For the situation of the hornet's nest style, you must be careful; without absolute certainty, it is best not to poke!

(18) Frequent Comparison (084)

Compare often. You will know the difference in level; understand others, understand yourself. People will suffer if they compare with others, and goods will be thrown away if they compare with others; if they die or are thrown away, what will be the use? Poor body, we have to compare with the worse; knowing that you are better off than many, you can get a safe work and rest. If you are physically strong, you have to compare yourself with stronger ones; knowing that you are worse off than some people, you have to try to make up for it. Look for flaws and make up for them; to be auspicious, develop more of your strengths! To determine the position, first look for the reference; tall and beautiful, close to the target, is the reference. A good search, from big to small; subtlety can be seen!

Chapter 4

(19) Encounter Things (085)

When things happen, don't be in a rush and get anxious; find the cause and solve the problem. Understand the truth and the right way, responsibility and interest; both sides have to stand in each other's shoes, to consider the problem. The three sides of the matter, the mutual need; cannot ban but to coordinate more. Good communication, to be on both sides of the parties involved; coordination does not work, and then reflect upwards to the superior, to further solve. People's mediation law needs to be promoted; mediation committee is a bridge between the two parties involved. Treat people with leniency and discipline yourself; control yourself, things will be perfect and complete!

(20) Take into Account the Big Picture (086)

To take into account the big picture, give up the small self; one must take into account the overall situation and seize the focus. A good way to deal with things is the view of golden mean; if things are extreme, they are bound to go the other way. When people have no choice, they may steal, cheat and rob; when the dog has no way, it may jump the wall in a hurry. Leave room for all to share! Leave a back road, we all share! Words are not to expressed out fully, things are not completely done; the heart is just, doing things is flexible and mobile. Morality should be wide, the law should be strict; with the rules, only to become a square circle. Condense consensus, gather strength; for the ideal, truly go create!

(21) In Leadership (087)

Destroy the leader, and the gang will collapse; why is it to do so? Because good or bad, it lies on the leader! In the team! In the party with which it is exchanged! A good leader takes the lead, supervises, and often manages to guide the right direction. Good teams are powerful; able to improvise and create endless frontiers. Some exchanges are like springs; if you are strong, it is weak; if you are weak, it is strong. There are shortcuts that are created by lazy people; becoming very diligent and busy now in order to save troubles later. The duck knows first when the river becomes warm in spring; to create goodness, you must rely on the frontline people to do it! Shut oneself up in a room making a cart - carry out one's idea irrespective of external circumstances, and it is difficult to fit; force others to sit, resentment will be a lot. Seek the same, save the differences, and design according to the actual needs. After thinking, designing and correcting again; finally, manufacture to satisfy the need!

(22) Rely on Yourself (088)

To be independent, one must depend on the distance; one is a separate individual and should not be too close to others. Relying on people requires return; one cannot save the poor and can hardly help the urgent. To guide the right way, rely on the truth; be self-reliant and self-sufficient; depend on yourself! Rely on yourself, and it is the cheapest; rely on yourself, and it is the most complete! To succeed, first, determine the goal; accumulate more, rise step by step. Know yourself and your opponent to determine the specific; right choice; do it step by step. Conform to the laws of heaven and earth, with the help of all forces; improvise, do things exclusively. Good timing, trade quickly; mutual satisfaction, common benefit. People have their own fate and luck, and the sky has unpredictable weather; the ship of ten thousand years relies on a right heart!

(23) For the Beginner's Mind (089)

For the sake of the beginner's mind, the will is strong; do it often, think about it often. Others sleep. I want to wake up early.

Chapter 4

Follow the plan, do not wait, and do not rely on others. Other people's flowers fall; mine has not yet blossomed; to use a little, create the future. Other people spend a day, and I use a year; to spend a lifetime, carrying out the realization. Day by day, slowly climbing; to reach the peak, the furnace. The mountain is not valued just by its height, and it is the immortals that bring its fame!Water is not valued just by its depth but by the dragon to make it alive! This bird, once it flies, will soar high into the sky; once it cries, it will startle the world with a single cry!Should one desire to sing, one would amaze the world with his first song!

(24) Fighting for the Honor (090)

No one cares, a worm; the worm turns into a giant dragon, and thousands of people welcome it. The rooster is crowing, the birds are laughing; the chicken becomes a phoenix, a hundred birds praise. If you have something, but don't have a disease!If you have nothing, but at least have capability! With power, there is hope; truly strong, to carry forward the good and the beautiful! For the sake of your family and country, for yourself; glorify your ancestors and return to your homeland with honor. People fight for the honour, Buddha fights for a pillar of incense; I want self-improvement, I want to advance upwards. Do my best to connect to the heaven and earth; to do what I have to do. A soldier who does not want to be a marshal is not a good soldier; stand straight and never mind if shadow inclines. The revolution has not yet succeeded, comrades still need to work hard; the heir of the dragon, to strive to be number one!

(25) Some people (091)

There are people who are simple at heart; straightforward and never act. There are people who love power; playing mind games with ulterior motives to the extreme. Subtle rules, how awesome; hanging a sheep's head, selling dog meat. Double standard is really irritating; regardless of oneself, focusing on others. Officials do management, businessmen do trade; a businessman conspire with the government, he is a fake and treacherous crook. A crooked stick will have a crooked shadow; if a leader sets a bad example, it will be followed by his subordinates; the little monk read the scriptures badly. The emperor is not worried, but his eunuchs are worried to death; the observers are more anxious than the person involved; The eunuch gets anxious but he has no right though! The ideal is beautiful, the reality is bleak; to achieve, you need three steps!

(26) I Hate You (092)

Emperor Xianfeng, I hate you!Why, did you cede the lands in the Outer Northeast? Yuan Shikai, I hate you!Why do you want to restore the imperial system? Chiang Kai-shek, I hate you!Why do you, lack justice? Some people, I hate you!Why do you, defy the law? There is no truth, lack of good creation; grieve yourself, future generations suffer. The great trend, who can resist? Even there are nine nines, they must eventually come to one! Extreme sensuality, mid-range rationality; the one who creates goodness righteously, is the most heroic of all! Where does the love come from? Where does hate come from? Goodness gets love!Sin gets hate!

(27) Heaven is Without Desire (093)

When heaven is free from desire, it will be naturally robust; and if a man has no desire, to what place does he go? There is a dream with the existence of desire; indeed, one will get what one wants. A girl will doll herself up for the man who loves her, and a gentleman will die for the patron who recognizes his worth; a man dies for his money, birds die in pursuit of food, and human beings die in pursuit of wealth. Even if you are beaten, you will come, and if you are scolded, you will go; without benefits, who will get up early? Proper selfishness should be carried forward; with the appropriate method, the country should escort. Let me pay, first to get; let me dedicate, first to self-protect! Like a clay idol fording a river, hardly able to save oneself, what to rely on to do good?

(28) Power is the Strength (094)

Power is a kind of strength, is a kind of management; power has benefits, but you must also give out. For those in power, responsibility interests to be tied, the people tomonitor; first by competition, then by election out. Public power is more weighty than the mountain; to manage, must share and divide power. Everyone has the right, and each manages; improve efficiency and be supremely fortunate. What should be managed is not managed; what should not be managed is managed instead; it is dead once it is managed, it is chaos when it is not managed. Everyone gives me rights; one must achieve actual creation, goodness, and beauty. For the people, no complaints; swear to God, no shame in my heart! First free, first to do; then find the problem, then management, then reform. Reform law should be established!Regulatory laws should be promoted! Propaganda of moral law should be in place; all kinds of lawsuits need to be handled for free!

(29) Good Talent (095)

Good talent, having the full range of abilities; one should understand the situation, and be well-versed in the opportunity to change. Without talents, it is difficult to develop; it is difficult to start a business, and even more difficult to keep a business. Use people without doubt, in doubt then not to use people; regularly supervising the management is the right action! Good talents can go up or down, can be bent or expanded; can detect the slightest change in things and know their development trends. One can understand the situation, two can summarize and calculate; three can propose a course of action, four can be specifically achieved. To be efficient, one needs to be small, fast, and ahead of schedule; to give and create correctly where no one else does!

(30) Running Owards Unity (096)

First of all, we need to personally possess, in order to be able to eat, wear and live; then the family is rich, and only then can we have wellbeing and happiness. First of all, we must be objective and fair, so that we can establish morality and law; then we can create and devote ourselves, so that we can have a beautiful country. The master is the proudest of all!Willing to be responsible and courageous to create! A good society is one in which people make the best use of their talents and things are distributed according to their work; a society that takes into account the disadvantaged. One, two, three, a step wider than a step; a walk in the clouds, like the sun. From the Republic of the Zhou Dynasty to the unification of the Qin Dynasty; from the departure of the Republic of China, to the establishment of the People's Republic of China. One heart, one mind, one power; revitalize China, run to unification!

(31) Buy, Lease, Borrow (097)

For the three situations of buying, leasing and borrowing, it is necessary to distinguish clearly; to make a decision according to the actual situation. With spare money, do not buy useless things; use the money to make money, it is the most cost-effective. You could afford and you use it frequently, so you choose to buy, feeling easy. Regardless of your affordability, the frequency of usage, choose to rent, it is most appropriateEasy to get in and out, and uncaring; no depreciation, feeling fine and balanced. Borrowing people's things, relying on favors; without that kind of human relations, you'd rather not to use, better not to borrow. If there is really no way, go ahead to borrow; do take more care of it, return early. If in case, something happens; one must compensate sincerely, have more communication!

(32) The Mass Psychology (098)

The mass psychology is really strange; the cheaper it is, the less they buy, the more expensive it is, the less they sell. Smart businessmen have many schemes; sell when it is expensive and buy goods to accumulate when it is cheap. All things need timing; without good timing, it is difficult to get benefits. To learn from the sage, Fan Li of the state of Chu; in more aspects, worked out miracles! The Chinese, who used to rely on agriculture and land; were often conservative and uninspired. The Jews, formerly uprooted; relied on business and are rich beyond measure. The English, French and Spanish, who valued industry and trade; their culture spread all over the world!

(33) A Thousand Mile Journey (099)

A journey of a thousand miles begins with a single step; things develop by osmosis. To eat, take one bite at a time; to speak, say one word at a time. To do something, start from small things; little by little, the big matter will become easy. To manage, start from the source; sort to do, simple and easy. When water has been flowing for a long time, it can drip through a stone; when people are dedicated for a long time, they can move a big mountain. The Poem for Today, says to do it today; the Song for Tomorrow, says to do it again tomorrow. The longer the night, the more dreams you have; when the timing is good, you can't delay, you must do it quickly! What is to be done today, do it well! What's for tomorrow, be ready today!

(34) Good Reputation (100)

A good reputation is a treasure; whoever gets it is good. Think first, then speak; say it and do it, do it and get results! A promise cannot be taken back once it is made, a word once out of the mouth cannot be overtaken by swift horses; a promise is weightier than one thousand bars of gold, it is never regretted. In case there is an emergency, and you can't do it, think of a way to tell in advance. Entrusted by others, devoted to others doing something; without confidence to complete it, do not offer the promise. If you don't keep your word, you are lying; no one will pay attention to it later, and it will be difficult for you to survive. To tell a lie, it must be in good intention; in order not to hurt others and to protect yourself. Borrow well, it is not difficult to borrow again; borrowed and not returned, there is no next time!

(35) For the Sake of Getting (101)

For the sake of gain, one devote selflessly; yet after gaining, change one's face. Without the truth, fake crookedness prevails; without creating good, evil appears. For the sake of enjoyment, there is a deliberate lack of supervision; each one does his own thing, and there is a great war of power. Family rich and prosperous, difficult to have three generations; the nation's life expectancy, difficult to have three hundred. Relay race, relying on talent; truly to create, good and beautiful will always be. Under the probe, who dares to break the law? Good regulation, good world! In ten cases, being fast for the nine times; Steady as you go, step by step!

(36) Two Roads (102)

There are two roads, which cannot be missing; the way in and the way out, both must be figured out. How to go, when and where? How to retreat, so as to suffer less? First consider

Chapter 4

the cons, then consider the pros!If you can't win, you have to bide your time! If you are strong, attack, if you are moderate, defend; if you are weak, retreat, if you are powerless, leave. There are people in the city who would love to be an officer; having the ability, connections and funds are the basic conditions for doing anything. If you are like an iron cock, too stingy to pull out a hair; it will be very difficult for you to do things. If you have remaining foods in your home, you will not panic; if you know a good number of martial arts, you will create wealth and happiness. Accumulate goodness into virtue, the holy heart is ready; accumulate trueness, create goodness and beauty!

(37) Man, Food and Clothes (103)

Man's food and clothing are the most necessary; if there is no plant, how to be fed? The well-being of man is the most important; if there is no more skin, how can there be hair? To truly create is the most important thing to do; without the fruits of creation, how to spend on buying? Without need, there is no good or bad; where does the result of good and beauty come from? The top is the manager, the middle is the processing craftsman; the bottom is the businessman, and the bottom is the cultivator. The people in the world are the lowest and the highest; without the civilian population, who can be good? A true man, needs to think; how to go about it, and everyone can be good!

(38) A River (104)

A river, long and deep and wide; the source of water is deep and flowing far. When it is in high tide, it does not flood; when it is in drought, the water flows continuously. A man, with good heredity; fundamentally strong, able to climb high. When one is young and learning, one is truly good; when one is adult, one creates a new high and go afar. To get the opportunity, must go to the challenge; good or bad, it is to judge and say by comparing

One Two Three

the ability. The road to happiness is full of hardships, good things are hard to come by; one needs to feel, needs to work hard. Adapt to external things, external things adapt to yourself; adapt to each other, it is the best way to get strength! Through the storm, see the rainbow; May your fortune be as boundless as the East Sea and your life last long like the South Mountain!

(39) One Palm (105)

One palm, it cannot be clapped; the responsibility of both sides, is not the same. When it's time to bow your head, don't lift it up; the water which became a sea by its low, a man became a king by his modesty. Give convenience to others, others will give convenience to yourself; to understand each other and look forward. Offense, defense and retreat, three aspects of nature; with a neutral exchange, the road is the widest! Both sides resist the war, both sides are wounded and disabled; the snipe and the clam fight, the fisherman gains. They come into unavoidable confrontation, the wise and brave win; when the realm of virtue becomes high, become friends. If water approaches, a dam is made from the earth, when the soldiers arrive we use a general to keep them off; it is the most justifiable being able to resolve it. To protect peace, the right side must be strong; while the priest climbs a post, the devil climbs ten. To develop, rely on supply and demand; complementary exchange is the most sustainable! A distant relative is not as good as a neighbor; being friendly with your neighbor makes you the happiest!

(40) Can I Do It (106)

Can things be done? Let's compare first! The amount of qualitative change that takes place determines the outcome! If you can reach it, or exceed it, it is possible to do it according to the plan. You cannot reach, or it is much smaller; better not, to taste the bitter fruit. When the time is right, harvest quickly; the actual ability determines their own degree of action, do not be greedy for more. The time is not ready, do not be anxious; look for the causes, make more efforts. If you are early, you have more opportunities; if you are late, you have less opportunities!Don't be late, be early! Take the initiative, it's the best!Be able to mobilize others, not be mobilized by others! There is nothing that can't be done, and there is no all-powerful thing to do; sometimes you just do not do it, but once you do it, you will surely win!

(41) Enjoying Labor (107)

If you love to do labor, everyone will respect you; if you love to do labor, you will be most glorious. If you are poor, you have to change; if you change, you will be able to adapt; if you want to adapt, you have to rely on labor. In order to produce, one must first work; after obtaining, one can use. After consuming, to grow ability; rely on the ability, feel life. Then turn ability into labor; create goodness and beauty, which are the most sacred. In labor, devote enthusiasm; feel relaxed, the most beautiful and happy. To forge iron, harden yourself; let people do it, first do it by yourself! Listen and obey to whoever arranges work as he is the one who employs or pays you, don't make your own decisions. ; if it is not correct, you should never do it! A gentleman loves wealth, take what you want; if it is not the right exchange to get, resolutely do not get it! Labor for a day, a night of peace of mind; hard work for a lifetime, eternal peace of mind!

(42) Supply (108)

The difference between supply and demand determines the market; whoever has the market, thrives. When supply is greater than demand, there will be the market for the demand side; when demand is greater than supply, there will be the market for the supply side. The balance of supply and demand, mutual benefit and a win-win situation; the country is prosperous and the people are at peace, the land yields good harvests and the people enjoy good health. The seller quotes the price, the buyer asks and sees; then exchange, reduce the trouble. Enter and exit the market according to the market prices; success or failure, reputation plays a major role. A clear accounting with confused ending; the same grade, no gap. Quality and price to adapt, the system is perfect; excellent circulation can make big money. He has none over me, and he has the advantage over me; having all of them, you can consider changing your career and turn away. The market is ruthless, and man has a heart; according to the need, go to the correct path. A good public plan needs the market economy to complete; the correct theory should take its place to be implemented!

(43) Small Calculations (109)

Small calculations, small goals; every family has a skeleton in the cupboard - each has its own problems. One likes two, two likes three; a love that can complement each other is hard to exchange with gold. The old like the young, the low like the high; the exchange of symmetrical extremes, is it wonderful? To be infinite, we must converge!To be the best, we need a superb leadership! The sky is high for the birds to fly, the sea is wide for the fish to leap; each gets his due, human beings are the best! A cosy nest is infinitely good; sleep and welcome the sunshine!

(44) All Things Prosper (110)

The good timing and geographical convenience are not as important as good human relations; when there is peace at home, everything will prosper! Because of little capability, not getting things done; when there is a mistake, prioritize in making peace! People in a great number will separate,dragons in large amount will make a mess; carry out unified management and action, you can reach the goal! When people have the same mind, it can

Chapter 5

break the gold; when people work together, the mountain can be moved. Individuals form families, families form nations; everyone creates, families flourish. One branch of the tree is particularly thriving- it is not spring; all flowers bloom together, that is the most charming. Accumulating abundantly and setting out properly; relying on correctness, honesty and good deeds, we can win the world!

Chapter 5

(1) One Person (111)

One person, walking one path; each person, not repeating. Eat three meals a day, wear a suit; sleep in a bed, occupy a piece of land. Don't pursue the external things outside ourselves too much; At birth we bring nothing; at death we take away nothing. Smile, a decade younger; worry turns the hair white. People are old, conservative and petty; old age is difficult. It is not easy to do things. Beauty on the outside, like flowers; only the truth, good and beauty are your callings! When you have money, how should you spend it? Doing charity is the best! While the world still belongs to you; spread love, make more efforts!

(2) Three Goals (112)

Three goals: life, career and love; human feeling consists of ten thousand kinds. Full load, feel the best; lack of load or overload, are the worst. If you need it, it smells sweet; if you don't need it, it smells bitter; if people are useless, they are like dung. If you want to get it, you should need it often; if you want to get joy and happiness, let the need be satisfied. Time is like an arrow, the day and the month are like a shuttle; time is golden and will not wait for me. If you have a wish, do it quickly; in the twinkling of an eye, you will be old. When it is appropriate, you will hand over the shift; when you are needed, you come to help more. What goes around, comes around; bring proactive to pay back is the blessing, passive to pay back is the scourge!

(3) **Planning for the World** (113)

To plan for all the ages, to plan for the whole situation; work out splendid plans to win victories in battles a thousand miles away. First plan for yourself, and then plan afar; lack of forbearance in small matters upsets great plans. If one is too selfish and place too much importance in the immediate future; it is difficult to achieve high and distant goals. There is heaven above, there is earth below; in the middle, there is myself. To do anything, we must first behave!To be a man in all honesty, to do something seriously! Face up to the conscience!Ancestors and descendants, keep them in mind! To abandon all falsehoods and evil!Do your best to create true goodness!

(4) **How to Walk** (114)

As one lives, how does one walk? One step, two steps, three steps, one step at a time to pursue. Living is not as good as it should be, what to do? To find a way, to change! No power to move forward, no place to go backward; to consolidate the roots, search for more. Behave in a low key manner, do things in a medium key manner; good nourishment in good times, and endure for creation in bad times. Too cold and too hot, are terrible; in the extreme place, do not settle down. The top earns from the bottom, the high positions manages the low positions; if the ability is great, move up! Be safe and healthy, get trained more; look for the time to create, and exchange with each other peacefully. When the scars are healed, the pain is forgotten; how can you act correctly if you do not endure to control? Be in control of your heart, open up your legs and move; learn to be true, create goodness and beauty!

(5) Want to Become Famous (115)

If you want to be famous, you must first be truthful; if you want to be renowned, you must create a contribution! Learn from the worker bee, picking flowers and making honey; learn from the stock master, grasping the right timing. Let people look for it, turn it into treasure first; comprehensive processing, meet the needs. The price is lower, the quality is better; the service is in place, the reputation is high. Create good and beautiful, compelling; for the people, more service! If you are excellent, others look for you; others are excellent; it is not easy to find. A granny sells melons, often praise themselves; if you are really good, who will be silly? If you are gold, you have to shine; learn Mao Sui, be brave to undertake responsibility!

(6) Have Faith (116)

With faith, one will not be lost; good faith, to truly create. Truly pursue, you will not regret; the best pursuit, create goodness and beauty. The highest state, is dignity; get dignity, no regret in life. One must first have the genuineness, then get the dignity; perfect dignity, must create goodness! The silkworm is dead while last silk ended. The candles burn into ash then only the tears dry. Zhuang Shiping, Xu Zengping, Bao Yugang, and Fok Ying Tung from Hong Kong; Wang Yongqing from Taiwan. Koo Tin Lok School, Run Run Shaw Building; the first philanthropist Cao Dewang, they love China, to be crowned with eternal glory.

(7) Multipolarization (117)

Multi-polarity is a law; like-minded people fall into the same group, things of a kind come together. To make a balance, that is also possible; solve the problem from the root. The reason for this is ability; the same ability, the difference is not much. The fundamental ability lies in the body; in the reality, in the opportunity. The low to learn high, high to help low; life concepts, to raise up. Life value, there are big and small; it could be heavier than a mountain, or lighter than a goose feather! The geese passed by and left a voice, a man passed by and left a reputation; correctly create good, shining in the history books!

(8) Have Good Steel (118)

With good steel, put it on the edge of the sword; with good powder, put it on your face. With food and clothing, go towards well-being; with genuineness, go to the creation of goodness and beauty. Life consists of a few decades, and it will be gone in the blink of an eye; what are you going to leave behind and dedicate to this place? Don't just say "I love you"!Your true goodness and beauty, where is it? The sunset is charming, only that it is near dusk; the sunrise is infinite beauty, only to move upwards. After this village, there is no such store; if you don't give, how long will you wait? Dedicate the most beautiful things to the one you love the most!In one's life, it is the most blissful! Give the best to those who need it most!In one's life, it is the most meaningful!

(9) Good Society (119)

A good society, slowly emerges; speaks of honesty and values the good environment. Improve from being passive to taking action; from sharing responsibility to voluntary commitment. With giving, there is gain; shares system is the most wonderful! Share the blessings and share the hardships; be down-to-earth and create brilliance. The former planted trees, the latter take advantage of the cool; drop of grace, never forget. Take it from the people, use it for the people; to use conscience, to be beautiful. People can control themselves, things can be automatic; do nothing and get the commonwealth!

(10) Core Concept (120)

Core concept,words; everyone likes it, everyone spreads it. Wealth, strength, democracy, civilization and harmony; freedom, equality, justice and rule of law. Patriotism and respect for work, honesty and friendliness; creating goodness and beauty, going high! The Five Principles, the moral rules between nations; Zhou Enlai's ability surpasses Zhuge Liang. Mutual respect for sovereignty and territorial integrity; non-aggression and non-interference in each other's internal affairs. Equality and mutual benefit, peaceful coexistence; true creation to ensure security and health! The people are the masters, the power is divided; the dragons rise up, who can compare? The Tibetan plateau is high, the Yangtze River and the Yellow River flow far away; wisdom of yesterday and today, tomorrow is infinite!

(11) What to Think About (121)

What to think about? What to do? To find problems!To solve problems and doubts! What do people live for? To pass down, to eat and be happy! Eating, drinking, being happy and living a long life would be the low and medium level pursuit; even if one could live for ten thousand years, eventually one would have to go. Passing down the people and culture is the most fundamental thing!It is the longest term, the highest depth! Without people, where comes the culture? Without people and culture, where comes the soul? A culture that truly creates goodness and beauty can help us move forward. We have to be the ladder, we have to be the bridge; for the dream, take it as our obligation! Easy come, easy go; how to do it, to be the most truthful?

(12) Passing on from Generation to Generation (122)

People, plants and animals and other things, constitute the

Chapter 5

system; to be harmonious, it is necessary to be dynamically balanced. Food, clothing, housing and transportation, well-being, happiness and true creation of goodness, need, stability and development; multiplicity, being cyclic. Creation and consumption, a matter of life and death!Limited resources, must be frugal! One person, three meals a day; hundreds of millions of people, the number of meals alone startles the earth and the sky. Falsehood, impropriety and waste, if exceeded the limits; the system will be chaotic and eventually lead to disaster. To die in peace and happiness is to be born in sorrow!Without distant worries, there will be near troubles! A family with many people, with capable people, takes on a heavy responsibility!The country has hundreds of millions of families that must be truly managed! Raise the quality and follow the nature!The population must be controlled so that it can be passed on from generation to generation!

(13) Three Hundred Thousand (123)

Three Character Classic, Hundred Family Surnames, Thousand Character Classic, Rules for Disciples; One Two Three, inherit the achievements of those who came before us and soar forward and upward. Please give me a real chance!I'm going to devote myself to truly creating goodness and beauty! Each family name sets up a society, help each other and learn from each other towards goodness and beauty. Tens of thousands of surnames, tens of thousands of societies; compete and develop, soar together. One Two Three, the establishment of the Foundation, will make the world become more beautiful. Nobel Prize, One Two Three prize; East and West, to compete virtuously and move forward. To build, One Two Three, a permaculture park; you and I, create together. Thought, planning and the actual action to do these steps are hard!Be accurate, decisive and brave. Victory comes today! A true star is not afraid of fire; it needs to shine and illuminate infinity. The good real, the beautiful creation of

One Two Three

goodness: the navigation of life, The One Two Three!

The pacific Ocean is big enough,
There's room for you, me and him.

太平洋，足够大；容得下，你我他

第一章

《一二三》

（1）天地人（001）

天是空，全包容；任万物，其中行。
地石土，是基础；天地合，万物出。
人精品，宇宙魂；守护神，是何人？

译文

天是空的，全部包容着万物；任凭万物在其中运行。
地是石头和土，是万物的基础；天地的合作，万物就产生了。
人是其中的精品，是宇宙的灵魂；守护宇宙的神灵，是什么样的人呢？

（2）你我它（002）

你我他，成一统；互制约，衡稳定。
我自己，你对面，他是三，和谐换。
它最广，它最繁；人外人，天外天！

译文

你我他组成一个系统；互相制约着，平衡而稳定。
我就是自己，你就是对面，他是第三者，我们要和谐地交换。
它最广大，它最繁多；人外面有人，天外面有天！

（3）昨今明（003）

昨今变，已不见；回不去，去怀念。
今明变，在眼前；不爱惜，后悔晚。
明未来，在何方？进不去，去向往！
昨今明，双向环；从远古，到近现！

译文

昨天是今天变的，已经不见啦；再也回不去，只有去怀念。
今天是明天变的，就在眼前；如果不爱惜而失去，再后悔就晚了。
明天还没有到来，它在哪里呢？我们进不去，只有去向往！
昨今明是双向循环的；它从远古时代，来到近代和现在！

《一二三》

（4）吃穿住（004）

吃为天，吃为地；是能源，是动力。
穿保护，穿保暖；为美观，为尊严。
住是休，住是眠；好睡眠，好今天。
行是走，行是动；真正行，必成功！
能是力，有目的；借方法，靠交易！

译文

吃就像天地一样重要；它就是能源，它就是动力。
穿为了保护，为了保暖；为了美观，为了尊严。
住就是休息，就是睡眠；有了好的睡眠，就有好的今天。
行就是走，就是动；真实正确的行动，必然会成功！
能是一种有目的的力量；它要借助方法，依靠交换才能实现目标！

(5)安康福(005)

安是全,己做主;常认真,无事故。
康是健,父母传;人健康,是本钱。
福安康,感舒享;有幸福,要向上。
乐得失,情欲放;善得乐,最理想!
寿是命,有短长;爱无限,寿无疆!

译文

安就是安全,由自己做主;经常认真,没有事故。

康就是健康,主要靠父母遗传;人健康,是做事的本钱。

福就是安全健康,感觉舒服享受;有了幸福,要积极向上。

乐就是得到和失去之后,感情欲望的释放;
善良得到快乐,是最理想的事情!

寿就是寿命,有短有长;奉献越多,寿命越长!

《一二三》

（6）真正创（006）

真客观，真规律；顺自然，不停息。
正中间，不歪偏；无真正，事难成。
创是换，是得到；少付出，多得到。
善是爱，是奉献；真正创，归于善。
美是好，是好感；日月星，照人间！
食与色，两本性；靠什么，去提升？

译文

真就是客观和规律；我们应该顺应自然，永不停息。

正就是在中间位置，不歪不偏；没有客观公正，做事难以成功。

创造就是交换，是一种得到；一种少的付出，多的得到。

善就是给别人爱，是一种奉献；真正创造之后，最后要奉献出去。

美就是美好，一种好的感受；就好像日月星辰，照亮人间一样！

食与色，是人的两种本性；要靠什么去提升它们，到达一个更高的境界呢？

第一章

（7）假歪费（007）

假是欺，假是空；假惺惺，不从容。
歪不正，偏离中；常扭曲，难正衡。
费失去，过度挥；正消费，不浪费。
恶是毒，是伤害；害别人，必自害。
丑难看，是坏感；勇面对，可变美！

译文

假就是欺骗，就是没有；虚情假意的人，是不会从容的。
歪就是不正，偏离中心；经常扭曲着，是难以公正平衡的。
费就是失去，一种过分的消费；要正确消费，不要浪费。
恶就是恶毒，是一种伤害；害了别人，自己必会受伤害。
丑就是难看，不好的感觉；勇于去改变，丑是可以变成美的！

《一二三》

（8）危病亡（008）

危是险，始下变；治未病，防未然。
病是变，失衡展；合理行，可扭转。
祸是害，已到来；知错改，从头来！
苦是难，天天感；得真知，献人间。
亡是死，变云烟；问耶稣，是何年？

译文

危就是危险，开始向不好的方向转变；要治未病，防患于未然。
病就是病变，失去平衡的发展；合理的行动，是可以扭转的。
祸就是祸害，已经到来了；知错就改，从头再来！
苦就是苦难，天天在感受着；要从中得到真理，奉献给社会。
亡就是死亡，变成了云烟；在天上问耶稣，现在是什么年代？

第一章

（9）数千年（009）

数千年，得精华；唯物论，辩证法。
厚载物，强不息；辩证一，是伏羲。
正治国，奇用兵；辩证圣，《道德经》。
《孙子法》，十三篇；其辩证，到顶点。
道可道，非常道！名可名，非常名！
天之道，利不害！人之道，为不争！

译文

人类在几千年中，得到的精华：就是唯物论和辩证法。

厚德载物，自强不息；发现辩证法的第一人，就是伏羲。

以正治国，以奇用兵；辩证法的圣典，就是《道德经》。

《孙子兵法》，共十三篇；对辩证法的运用，达到了一个顶点。

道是可以说的，但不是一般的道理！名是可以说明的，但不是一般的名！

天道就是，有利于万物而无害！人道就是，有所作为而不争名夺利！

《一二三》

（10）汉字创（010）

汉字创，文明光；容开放，传万方。
帮记事，帮思想；助科哲，助正创。
语同声，字同样；统一便，向前上！
中文学，数篇名；细品味，如临境。
片冰心，在玉壶；有灵犀，一点通。
千金去，还复来；生我材，必有用！
刘禹锡，《陋室铭》；周敦颐，爱莲情。
《岳阳楼》，乐与忧；《醉翁亭》，不在酒。
姜《六韬》，儒《经书》；荀《劝学》，《墨子》术。
《春夜雨》，《鹳雀楼》；原上草，人长久！

译文

汉字创造了，文明的光芒；包容开放，传向万方。
帮助记事，帮助思想；帮助科学哲学，帮助正确地创造。
语言同声，文字同样；统一方便，向前向上。
中国文学，很多篇有名气；细细品味，如临其景。
一片冰心在玉壶；心有灵犀一点通。
千金散去还复来；天生我材必有用！
刘禹锡，写了《陋室铭》；周敦颐，写了《爱莲说》，倾诉爱莲之情。
《岳阳楼记》说的是，先天忧，后天乐；《醉翁亭记》，醉翁之意不在酒。
姜尚的《六韬》，儒家的《经书》；荀子的《劝学》，《墨子》的技术。
《春夜喜雨》，《登鹳雀楼》；离离原上草，但愿人长久！

第一章

（11）东方亮（011）

东方亮，太阳出；布德泽，万物苏。
中文化，博大深；中语文，勇创新。
组分便，易知意；好工具，数第一。
精简用，易传承；冉冉起，东文明。
繁长平，难流通；渐渐去，西文明。
谁先进，谁标准；高效率，吸引人。
高科技，大实力；正人文，领统一。
东西方，要统一；靠中国，靠汉语。
中国兴，世界起；地球村，文明地。
勺子西，筷子东；早晚勺，筷中兴！

译文

东方亮啦，太阳出来啦；散布德泽，万物复苏。
中国文化，博大精深；中国语言文字，勇于创新。
组分方便，容易知意；好的工具，它数第一。
精简实用，容易传承；冉冉升起，东方文明。
由于繁长平淡，难以流通；西方的文明，渐渐地失去了。
谁先进，谁定标准；效率越高，越吸引人。
高的科技，大的实力；正确的人文，引领统一。
东西方，要想统一；要靠中国，要靠汉语。
中国兴旺啦，世界就起来啦；地球村，就会变成文明的地方啦。
勺子在西方，筷子在东方；老少用勺子，筷子中年兴！

第二章

《一二三》

（1）一二三（012）

一二三，搬金砖；三二一，步步低。
人从众，是民主；众从人，一人主。
口吕品，大家尝；品吕口，个人享。
日昌晶，群星耀；晶昌日，太阳照。
子孖孨，人多患；孨孖子，中美健！

译文

一步两步三步，就可以搬金砖；从三步到两步到一步，一步比一步低小。

个人服从大众，就是民主；大众服从个人管理，就是一人做主。

一口两口三口，大家品尝；从多口到一口，个人享用。

从一星到多星，群星闪耀；从多星到一日，太阳照射。

从一子到多子，人多为患；从多子到一子，只有不多不少，才是最美好健全的！

第二章

（2）出于蓝（013）

出于蓝，胜于蓝；一二三，系双环。
一生二，二生三；三生万，反向变。
一状态，固液气；二性能，阴阳中。
三主次，主客辅；四渐进，匀加速。
五顺序，祖父己；六方法，三步棋。
七结构，夫妻子；八功能，优中次。
九系统，恒行卫；十循环，三十年！

译文

青出于蓝而胜于蓝；一二三，在系统中双向循环。

一变二，二变三；三生万物，然后就会向相反的方向改变，越来越少。

第一是状态，有固态，液态，气态；第二是性能，有阴性，阳性，中性。

第三是主次，有主次辅三种；第四是渐进，比如均匀地加速。

第五是顺序，从祖父到父亲到自己；第六是方法，有三步走的方法。

第七是结构，家庭中包括丈夫，妻子和孩子；第八是功能，有优中次三种。

第九是系统，恒星系包括恒星，行星和卫星；第十是循环，有时候是三十年。

《一二三》

（3）辩证律（014）

辩证律，一二三；明其理，大道简。
一物体，难运动；多物换，成事情。
两物换，得结果：大小等，有一种。
绝对值，会相等，结果和，等于0。
成交量，最小量，换系数，参量乘。
聚散量，度时乘，度与时，反向行。
大宇宙，小天地；归根底，0和一！

译文

辩证交换定律有三个；明白其中的道理，大道理就很简单。

一个物体是难以运动的；多个物体的交换就变成了事情。

两物交换得到的结果：有大于，小于和等于三种结果之一种。

它们的绝对值相等，双方结果之和等于0。

成交量一般是双方中的最小量，是交换系数和参与量的乘积。

物体的聚散量等于交换程度与时间的乘积；数量一定，程度与时间成反比。

大的宇宙，小的天地；归根结底都是0和一。

（4）物三端（015）

物三端，两对称；好中调，暖人心。
物三态，性三面；条件变，会转换。
一状态，一性能；三态性，单一行。
特殊性，尺有长；普遍性，小于丈。
异性吸，同性排；互相需，难分开。
物结构，定性能；三角形，最稳定！
系统素，最少三；少于三，难循环。
石剪布，成循环；环制环，单向前。
各环节，都关键；最要命，薄渡环！

译文

物体的三端，有两端对称；好的中端调节，温暖人心。
物体有三种状态，三种性能；条件改变，就会改变。
一种状态，一种性能；三种状态性能，一般只存在一种。
物体的特殊性，尺有所长；在普遍性中，尺是小于丈的。
异性相吸，同性相排；两性互相需要，难以分开。
物体的结构，决定性能；三角形的结构，是最稳定的。
组成系统的要素，最少需要三个；少于三个，是难于循环的。
石头，剪子，布，组成的循环；一环制约另一环，并且是向一个方向前进的。
各个环节都是关键环节；最要命的，是薄弱和过渡的环节！

《一二三》

（5）先观察（016）

先观察，后思考；先积累，后分类。
综合析，找规律；守安康，背危亡。
三推理，类归绎；因果律，最简易。
因生果，果生因；因果环，周期变。
善善报，恶恶报；不不报，时未到！
个组整，整分散；慢时长，快时短。
要时短，就要快；要长在，慢慢来。
己慢快，它快慢；己正稳，感未变。
一二三，三二一；四五六，七八九。
事发展，如波浪；底整合，随后旺！

译文

先观察，然后思考；先积累材料，然后再分类。
综合分析，寻找规律；守规律就安康，不遵守就危亡。
三种推理，类比，归纳和演绎；因果规律是最简易的。
因产生果，果又产生新的因；因果循环，就会出现周期性变化。
善有善报，恶有恶报；不是不报，时间未到！
个体组成整体，整体分散成个体；慢了时间就长，快了时间就短。
要时间短，就需要快；要长时间存在，就慢慢来。
自己慢了或快了，感觉其它就快了或慢了；自己正常稳定，感觉没有变化。
一二三，三二一；四五六，七八九。
事情的发展，如同波浪一样；在底部整合，随后就旺盛起来！

（6）知其然（017）

知其然，所以然；一反三，万物连。
纯则真，干则净；中则正，机则动。
解铃者，系铃人；要止沸，先抽薪。
要求稳，低重心；谦受益，满招损。
先求安，后求胜；先退让，后冲锋。
牵一发，动全身；全过程，要认真。
石问路，三思行；砖引玉，提衣领。
走一步，看多步；用好物，早铺路。
前面车，后面辙；摸石头，去过河！
当者迷，旁者清；偏则暗，兼则明！

译文

知道这样，知道为什么这样；举一反三，万物相连。
纯了就真，干了就净；在中间就正，有机会就会动。
解铃的人，有时就是系铃的人；要想止沸，应该先抽去薪火。
如果要求稳，需要重心低。谦虚得到益处，自满招来损失。
要先求安，然后再求胜；要先退让，然后再冲锋。
牵一发而动全身；整个过程，一定要认真。
投石问路，三思而后行；抛砖引玉，提衣服，先拿衣领。
走一步，看多步；用好的外物，预先铺好道路。
前面有车，后面有辙；摸着石头去过河！
当局者迷，旁观者清；偏听则暗，兼听则明！

《一二三》

（7）时连续（018）

时连续，空广延；时空合，物机现。
可同时，可同地；时空变，无同机。
物越大，机越小；物与机，成反比。
物机遇，分多样：好合作，坏战抗。
缺和余，是前提；换时空，是机遇。
两物体，能互补；合作件，才满足。
好系数，好时空；供需换，事事兴。
找时机，找缺余；满缺余，创时机！
《小池》诗，杨万里；一蜻蜓，善握机！

译文

时间就是物体的连续存在性，空间就是物体的广延存在性；两者结合，物体的机会就会出现。

有同时，有同地；由于时空的改变，没有相同的两个机会。

物体越大，机会越小；物体的体积与机会成反比。

物体的机会分为多种多样：好的是合作，坏的是战抗。

缺和余是构成机会的前提条件；进行交换的时间空间就是机会。

两个物体能够互相补充；合作的条件才会满足。

好的交换系数，好的时空；供需交换，事事兴旺。

找时机，先找缺余；满足缺余，创造时机。

《小池》诗的作者是杨万里；诗中那只蜻蜓，很善于把握时机！

(8) 间接换 (19)

任何换, 间接换; 需中介, 帮实现。
有能者, 无特殊; 只不过, 善借物。
善其事, 利其器; 靠人才, 创第一。
站得高, 望得远; 借好物, 能发展。
好外物, 像翅膀; 正交换, 任飞翔。
挑外物, 要达标; 高性能, 低消耗。
选人才, 身体好; 德能美, 善言表!

译文

任何交换, 都是间接交换; 需要中介物帮助, 才能实现。
有能力的人, 没有什么特殊; 只不过善于借助外物罢了。
工欲善其事, 必先利其器; 依靠好的人才, 才能创造第一。
站得高, 才能望得远; 借助好的外物, 才能发展。
好的外物, 就像翅膀一样; 与之正确地交换, 任你飞翔。
挑选外物, 一定要达标; 其中包括高性能, 低消耗。
选用人才, 身体一定要好; 有德有能又美, 善于言表!

《一二三》

（9）温水物（020）

温水物，草树出；木水换，动物现。
物进化，亿万年；人出现，站顶端！
植物善，动物天；造氧气，吃住穿。
动物简，缺心眼；不换衣，不打扮。
人金贵，最麻烦；生死间，事连连。
众植物，如爹娘；没它们，谁来养？
众动物，如兄妹；没它们，谁来陪？
万事物，都有命；多爱惜，求共生！
物植动，人为峰；到顶端，向下行！

译文

合适的温度，水和物质混合，草树就会生出；草木同水的交换，动物就会出现。

动物进化了亿万年；人出现之后，慢慢地站到了顶端！

植物善良，是动物的天；制造氧气，吃的，住的和穿的。

动物简单，缺少心眼；不换衣服，也不打扮。

人最金贵，人最麻烦；生死之间，事连连。

众多的植物，如同爹娘一样；没有它们，谁来养我们？

众多的动物，如同兄弟姐妹一样；没有它们，谁来陪伴我们？

万事万物，都有生命；要多爱惜，寻求共同生活！

从物质到植物再到动物，人是最高峰；人到了顶端，就会向下运行，最后回到起点！

第二章

（10）世界观（021）

世界观，人观点；方法论，如何换。
唯物论，说客观；辩证法，指实践。
物能信，存一身；物信表，能是魂。
物能换，信息现；物物换，万物变。
有朝霞，不出门；火烧云，晒死人。
燕低飞，蛇溜道；有大雨，不久到。
想办法，喝口水；洗好手，全靠嘴。
油开后，晾一晾；少污染，炒菜香。
吃完饭，倒点水；刷刷碗，漱漱嘴。
肚里疼，不用急；解解手，放放气！

译文

世界观就是人的观点；方法论就是怎样交换。
唯物论说的是客观；辩证法是用来指导实践的。
物质，能量和信息，三者合为一体；物质，信息是外表，能量是灵魂。
物质与能量交换，信息就出现；物体与物体交换，万物就变化。
早上有彩云，可能下雨，不要出门；傍晚有红云，明天可能会很热。
燕雀低飞蛇溜道，大雨不久就来到。
想办法，喝一口水；把手洗好，全靠嘴的控制。
油烧开后，晾一晾；然后再炒菜，污染少，菜又香。
吃完饭后，碗里倒点开水；先刷刷碗，再淑淑嘴。
肚里疼痛，不要着急；解解大手，排排气，也许就好啦！

《一二三》

（11）动生换（022）

动生换，生量变；到时间，就质变。
为平渡，防烈变；靠改革，调量变。
得平衡，动态环；到程度，又始变。
知方向，得趋势；大趋势，知大概。
一三一，知高低；好预测，知未来。
必然事，提前备；偶然事，多应对。
要防火，要防贼；防不测，防溺水。
要完善，早打算；事超前，备无患！
蚁憾树，不自量；大堤毁，何感想？

译文

运动产生交换，交换产生数量的变化；到了一定时间，就会发生质的变化。

为了平稳过渡，防止剧烈变化；需要依靠改革，调整量变。

得到平衡后，开始进行动态循环；到了一定的程度，又会开始量变，质变。

知道了方向，就知道发展趋势；大的趋势，了解大概。

昨天的高低，可判断今天的高低；正确的预测，可知未来的真实情况。

必然的事情，要提前准备；有可能的事情，要多方面准备。

要预防着火，贼偷；预防想不到的和被水淹没。

要想完善，就要提前打算；做事超前，有备无患！

蚂蚁撼大树，可笑不自量；当大堤被蚂蚁毁掉的时候，有何感想呢？

第二章

（12）人遗传（023）

人遗传，定身体；身代谢，定活力。
人活力，定趣好，定性格，定能标。
人能力，定人生，定境界，活业情。
望闻知，思想定；身去行，心感应。
知真实，定正道；行创善，感美好。
华盛顿，一总统；真英明，万古青。
一介石，蒋中正；行假歪，留骂名。
飞鸟尽，藏良弓；知进退，善始终！

译文

人的遗传，决定了人身体的好坏；身体的代谢程度，决定了活力的大小。

人的活力，决定了人的兴趣和爱好；决定了性格，决定了能力和目标。

人的能力，决定了人的一生；决定了境界，生活，事业和爱情。

看听之后便知，思想之后做决定；靠身体去行，靠心灵去感受。

知道真实之后，确定正道；去创造，奉献之后，感受美好。

华盛顿，美国第一任总统；真正英明，万古长青。

字为介石的，蒋中正；说假话，做歪事，留下千古骂名。

飞鸟没了，弓箭就没有用了；要知道正确的进退，才能够善始善终！

《一二三》

（13）人自己（024）

人自己，最重要；没自己，全完了。
人私有，最可靠；没私有，人心跑。
先自己，后周边！先私有，后高端！
丢自己，崇媚外；帮数钱，被人卖。
敌人友，敌人敌；友或敌，正分析。
有永己！有永利！没永友！没永敌！
爱自己，爱对方；爱他方，共成长。
心如海，万花开；真正创，善美来！

译文

人自己，是最重要的；没有自己了，对自己来说，就全完了。

人自己拥有，是最可靠的；没有私有，人和心就跑了。

要先自己，然后再说周边！要先私有，然后再说高端的公有等事情！

丢掉自己，崇洋媚外；帮人数钱，已被人卖。

敌人的朋友，敌人的敌人；到底是朋友还是敌人，要正确地去分析。

有永远的自己！有永远的利益！没有永远的朋友！没有永远的敌人！

要爱自己，要爱对方；要爱第三方，要共同成长。

心如大海，万花常开；客观公正地去创造和奉献，美好就会到来！

（14）私与公（025）

私与公，个与整；互转化，互作用。
私是人，要财物；要自由，要平等。
公家团，党政国；公权力，监管理。
为了私，组成公；帮护私，公作用。
不爱私，公何用？不爱公，家国零。
要富国，先富民！要强国，先强军！
私爱公，从我起！公完美，我得利！
私变公，靠正善！公变私，靠正换！

译文

私和公，是个体和整体的关系；它们互相转化，互相作用。

私就是个人，需要财物；需要自由，需要平等。

公就是家庭，团体，政党，政府和国家；公就是公共权力，监督和管理。

为了更好地私有，才组成了公有；帮助保护私有，是公有最基本的作用。

如果公不爱私，要公有什么用呢？如果私不爱公，家国就会破碎飘零。

要想富国，先要富民！要想强国，先要强军！

私爱公，从我做起！公完美了，我就会得到好处！

把私有变为公有，靠的是公正善良！把公有变为私有，靠的是正确地交换！

《一二三》

（15）施仁政（026）

施仁政，像春风；万物生，事事通。
行暴政，似寒冬；物凋零，困重重。
汉文景，唐太宗；因仁政，空前荣。
秦赵高，隋杨广；因暴政，转眼亡。
一刀切，背真理；野蛮行，怨恨起。
靠惩罚，达目的；成不足，败有余。
问大众，定德律；正执法，大欢喜。
不约同，异同声；大趋势，已形成。
大趋势，要看清；早布局，稳顺应。
多竞争，少垄断！自动化，最自然！

译文

施行仁政，就像春风一样；万物生长，事事通顺。
施行暴政，就像寒冬一样；万物凋零，困难重重。
汉朝的文帝景帝，唐朝的李世民；因为仁政，空前繁荣。
秦朝的胡亥，隋朝的杨广；因为暴政，转眼而亡。
一刀切做事，违背真理；野蛮执行，怨恨四起。
依靠惩罚，达到目的；成事不足，败事有余。
询问大众后，再确定道德法律；公正执法，皆大欢喜。
如果出现不约而同，异口同声；大的趋势，就已经形成啦。
大的趋势，一定要看清；要早早布局，稳稳顺应。
要多一些竞争，少一些垄断！自动化，是最自然的！

（16）万物生（027）

万物生，靠天地；靠日月，靠规律。
顺自然，顺规律；得真正，得美息。
毁林猎，竭泽渔；难复原，害人己。
为眼前，灭山基；变干旱，沙尘起。
美尧山，成过去；变尧坑，无人理！
年损失，难以计；靠卖面，去充饥。
莫失去，勿遮蔽；山水树，旷神怡！
好自然，像汉语；丰富多，让人迷！

译文

万物生长，依靠天地；依靠日月，依靠自然规律。
要顺应自然现象，顺应自然规律；才能得到真正，得到美好的安息。
毁林而猎，竭泽而渔；难以恢复原状，害人害己。
为了眼前利益，把山脉变成平地；天气变干旱，沙尘四起。
美丽的尧山，变成了过去；变成了深坑，无人理会！
每年的损失，难以计算；当地人，靠卖方便面维持生活。
莫要失去，不要遮蔽；山水树木，让人心旷神怡！
好的自然，就像汉语一样；丰富多彩，让人着迷！

《一二三》

（17）万事物（028）

万事物，皆工具；互换用，向前去。
宇万物，各不同；按规律，系中行。
新陈谢，光合用；核聚变，氧反应。
物能信，成世界；科哲文，成学业。
对立面，矛盾换；从对抗，到战商。
多则分，少则聚；最美时，是中期！
有开始，就有终；最美好，是过程！
整绝对，个相对；整统一，个美丽！

译文

万事万物，都是工具；互相交换利用，向前面走去。
宇宙万物，各不相同；按照规律，在系统中运行。
有新陈代谢，光合作用；有核聚变，氧化反应。
物质，能量和信息，组成世界；科学，哲学和文学，组成学业。
对立的两面，既矛盾又交换；从对立，抗拒，到战斗，协商。
多了就分开，少了就聚集；最美好的时间是中期！
有了开始，就有终点；最美好的就是过程！
整体是绝对的，个体是相对的；整体统一，个体美丽！

第二章

（18）创系统（029）

创系统，方法论；吴孙子，第一人。
从战略，到战术；《孙子法》，系统述。
定目标，让人屈；借外物，道天地。
知己彼，重自己；合理划，庙堂里。
循序进，逐个击；随机变，命不理。
握时机，实击虚；卒善养，后善理。
知己难，正行难；真正创，善最难！
知彼难，交换难；成知心，最困难！
大能者，何来难？治大国，若烹鲜！

译文

创造了系统方法论；春秋吴国的孙武，是第一个人。
从战争的谋略，到战争的方法；《孙子兵法》，进行了系统的论述。
确定目标，让人屈服；借助外物，道法，天时，地利等。
知己知彼，重视自己；在庙堂里，合理筹划。
循序渐进，逐个击破；随机应变，君命不理。
把握时机，避实击虚；投降的士兵，好就留着，最后做好善后工作。
认识自己难，正确行动难；真正创造后，奉献最难！
认识对方难，合理交换难；变为知心朋友，最困难！
有大能力的人，哪里来的困难呢？治理大的国家，就像烹饪小鲜一样简单！

《一二三》

（19）留山水（030）

留山水，植物美；动物人，能消费。
合理费，满需要；适生产，系统好。
费付出，费得到；费转换，费目标。
物三类，产四类；到最后，变消费。
一物质，二能量，三信息，共三样。
一工业，二运业，三商业，四管业。
工运销，费回产；智管理，循发展！

译文

留下山水，植物就美；动物和人，能够消费。
合理消费，满足需要；适当生产，系统完好。
消费是付出，消费是得到；消费是转换，消费是目标。
物体分三类，产业分四类；到最后，变成消费。
第一是物质，二是能量，三是信息，共三样。
第一产业是工业，二产业是运输业，三是商业，四是管理业。
加工，运输，销售，消费，回收和再生产；需要智能管理，循环发展！

第二章

（20）留智能（031）

留智能，万年青；无遗症，感轻松。
傻人类，别太精！不能留，后遗症！
玻璃体，被破碎；伤人物，谁之罪？
塑料品，到处扔；太平洋，不太平。
植物死，动物亡；人生活，难保障。
人造物，虽方便；难分解，堆成山。
不回收，不再产；不循环，成灾难。
要良展，必良环；重回收，重再产。
有此品，必能解；不环保，禁流产！

译文

留下智慧能力，万年长青；没有后遗症，感觉轻松。
傻傻的人类，不能过于精明！不能给后人，留下后遗症！
玻璃的物体，被人破碎；伤害人和其它物，是谁的罪过呢？
塑料物品到处扔；太平洋变得不太平。
有的植物死了，有的动物亡了；人的生活难以得到保障。
人造物品，虽然方便；有的难易分解，堆积如山。
不回收，不再次生产；不循环了，就会造成灾难。
要想良好地发展，必须良好地循环；必须重视回收，重视再生产。
有了这种物品，必须能够分解它；不环保，禁止流通与生产！

《一二三》

（21）想得到（032）

想得到，无厚非；只要你，不违背。
得就失，失就得；得失正，心平衡。
谁付出，谁得到；谁得到，谁三包！
谁做错，谁挽回！勇承担，不后悔！
卖塑品，收塑料；卖物品，收外包。
有垃圾，要分类；循环用，无限美。
站中间，顾前后；废入坑，纸入篓。
不强制，最真实；看如何，去公厕！

译文

要想得到，无可厚非；只要你不违背，道德和法律就可以。
得到就失去，失去就得到；得失公正，心理平衡。
谁付出了，谁就得到；谁得到了，谁就三包！
谁做错了，谁去挽回！勇于承担，不会后悔！
卖塑料物品的，要回收旧塑料；卖物品的，要回收物品的外包装。
有了垃圾，一定要分类；循环利用，无限美好。
站在中间，顾及前后；废物入坑，手纸入篓。
不进行强制，是最真实的；看真实情况，去公共厕所就可以啦！

第二章

（22）从从从（033）

从点线，到全面；有量变，才质变。
从积土，到成山；有基础，才高端。
从内部，到外形；好结构，好性能。
从个人，到系统；要发展，必良争。
从主观，到客观；按规律，去发展。
从个体，到普遍；先真正，后创善。
从联盟，到家国；从党国，到共和！

译文

从点到线，到整个平面；有了数量的变化，才会有性质的改变。

从逐渐积土，到成为土山；有了下面的基础，才会有上面的高端。

从内部情况，到外部形态；有了好的内部结构，才会有好的外部性能。

从一个人，到一个系统；要想发展，必须良性竞争。

从个人观点，到真实情况；要按照规律，去发展。

从个体现象，到普遍规律；首先要客观公正，然后才能创造奉献。

从部落到联盟到家国；从党国之后到达共和国！

第三章

《一二三》

（1）金木水（034）

金銮鑫，像海水；鑫銮金，稀为贵。
木林森，贵如今；森林木，不见树。
水沝淼，龙门跳；淼沝水，物离飞。
火炎焱，烈火烧；焱炎火，小火苗。
土圭垚，风雨飘；垚圭土，沙尘暴！

译文

金子越来越多，就像海水一样不值钱；金子越来越少，物以稀为贵。
从树少到树多，就像今天一样美好；从树多到死木，再也看不见活树了。
水越来越多，会出现鱼跳龙门；水越来越少，动植物就会离开飞走。
小火到大火，烈火燃烧；大火到小火，只剩小火苗。
土变山，风雨飘扬；山变土，会出现沙尘暴！

第三章

（2）不吃穿（035）

不吃穿，怎住行? 不住行，怎有能?
不有能，怎安康? 不安康，怎福乐?
不福乐，怎长寿? 不长寿，怎真正?
不真正，怎创善? 不创善，怎美好?
学得真，思得正；行得创，慈善良！
先硬件，后软件；合正力，去创善！

译文

不吃穿，怎么住行呢？不住行，怎么有能呢？

没有能，怎么安康呢？没有安康，怎么福乐呢？

没有福乐，怎么长寿呢？不长寿，怎么真正呢？

不真正，怎么创善呢？不创善，怎么美好呢？

学习得到真，思考得到正；靠行动得创造，创得慈，慈得善，善得良！

先有硬件，后有软件；合成正力，去创善！

《一二三》

（3）什么事（036）

什么事，可以做？什么话，可以说？
利人己，可说做！害人己，不说做！
万事物，有规则；人遵守，法与德。
真正美，德法魂；换得失，不矛盾。
人道德，分三样；低中高，步步尚。
好道德，自觉守；有人背，靠众口。
好法律，必真正；谁跨越，必严惩！
都守德，律不用；各得所，人人圣。
我错了，对不起！原谅你，没关系！
你助我，谢谢你！互相助，不客气！

译文

什么事情，可以去做？什么言语，可以去说？

有利于别人和自己的，可以去说，去做！害人害己的，不能说和做！

万事万物的运行，都是有规则的；人要遵守法律和道德。

真正创善美是道德，法律的灵魂；在交换时，得到和失去，平衡不矛盾。

人的道德分三样；从低到中到高，一步比一步高尚。

对好的道德，要自觉遵守；有人违背，靠大家说话制止。

好的法律，必须客观公正；谁跨越了，必须严惩！

都遵守道德，法律不使用；各得其所，人人高尚。

我错了，就说，对不起！原谅你啦，就没关系！

你帮助我，就说，谢谢你！我们互相帮助，不客气！

第三章

（4）越前山（037）

越前山，到后天；无后大，孝为先！
君管臣，父管子，夫管妻，三纲理。
齐管仲，四维立：说廉耻，道礼义。
孔孟董，定五常：仁义礼，智信起。
吴孙子，五事宜：将与法，道天地。
好将才，五条件：智信仁，勇与严。
旧社会，五德讲：温良恭，俭与让。
德报德，直报怨；犯我者，远必诛！

译文

越过前面的山，到达其后面的天；无后为大，百善孝为先！
君主管大臣，父亲管儿子，丈夫管妻子，是三纲的道理。
齐国的管仲，确立了四维：廉耻礼仪。
孔子，孟子和董仲舒，确立了五常：仁义礼智信。
吴国孙武，定五事：道天地将法。
好将才的五个条件是：智信仁勇严。
旧社会，讲五德：温良恭俭让。
以德报德，以直报怨；侵犯我的人，虽然远，也必须惩罚！

《一二三》

（5）悠悠地（038）

悠悠地，悠悠天；敬万物，人灿烂。
瓜得瓜，豆得豆；好管理，好丰收。
一先天，父母担；孕育前，必安健。
二家园，是后天；好家庭，美校园。
三入会，共监管；好生活，自实现。
先吃穿，后住行；先能力，后理立。
最大敌，是自己；管好己，事如意。
要成功，先设计；借外物，靠能力。
自始终，一条龙；国战略，应力行！

译文

悠悠的地，悠悠的天；尊敬万物，人最灿烂。
种瓜得瓜，种豆得豆；有好的管理，就有好的丰收。
第一是出生前，靠父母承担；孕育之前，必须安全健康。
第二是家庭和校园，是后面的因素；需要好的家庭，美的校园。
第三是进入社会，大家要共同监管；好的生活，要靠自己去实现。
首先要吃穿合理，然后要住行得当；先有能力，然后自理，自立。
最大的敌人是自己；管好自己，做事如意。
要想成功，先要设计；借助外物，依靠能力。
对一个人，自始至终要一条龙服务；这是国家战略，应大力推行！

第三章

（6）从一起（039）

好想好，来不了；遗传病，添烦恼。
我命运，谁来定？父母亲，定输赢！
人父母，无意中；其子女，苦一生。
从遗传，到营养；从教育，到成长。
子女命，握手中！怀孕前，先验种！
无良种，不下地！无能力，不生育！
起跑线，在这里！最重要，最急需！
育基金，育康院！为后代，无私献！
人家国，快注意！为二三，从一起！

译文

我好想好啊，可是来不了；父母遗传的疾病，增添了我的烦恼。
我的命运，谁来决定？是父母亲，决定了输赢！
人的父母，在无意之中；他们的子女，有可能会痛苦一生。
从遗传因素，到营养因素；从教育因素，到其他成长因素。
子女的命运，握在父母手中！怀孕之前，需要先检验种子是否良好！
没有好的种子，就不要盲目下地！没有能力，就不要生育！
真正的起跑线，是在这里！这是最重要的，这是最急需要去做的！
国家需要成立生育基金，需要成立生育健康医院！为了后代，要无私奉献！
个人，家庭和国家，要尽快注意！为了二和三，要从一做起！

《一二三》

（7）糖尿患（040）

糖尿患，最苦难！人间狱，苦难言！
看外表，很健全；谁知里，太遗憾。
心无力，趣好淡；身无力，只听看。
心凄凄，路漫漫；谁人知？谁人关？
这慈善，那慈善；为什么，不靠前？
想归想，现归现；自苦难，自来感。
山穷尽，疑无路；柳花明，在何处？

译文

糖尿病患者，是最苦最难的！犹如人间地狱，有苦难言！
看外表，是很健全的；谁知内里，太让人遗憾啦。
内心无力，兴趣，爱好平淡；身体无力，只能听看，无法去做。
心里凄凉，道路漫长；哪个人知道呢？又有谁去关心呢？
这个慈善，那个慈善；为什么，不靠前帮助一下呢？
思想归思想，现实归现实；自己的苦难，只有自己来感受。
山穷水秀疑无路；柳暗花明，在何处？

第三章

（8）太大意（041）

年轻时，太大意；为挣钱，伤身体。
中年后，病缠身；好感觉，无处寻。
人久病，乱投医；吃药多，伤元气。
一步错，步步错；至今日，难自我。
人痛苦，也是福！苦资源，好好读！
人一生，为感想；人活着，有希望！
现在起，从我起！养生息，东山起！
黎明前，夜凄凉；无奈中，盼孙阳！
越苦想，越漫长；创造中，见曙光！

译文

年轻的时候，太大意啦；为了挣钱，伤了身体。
到了中年，疾病缠身；好的感觉，无处去寻。
人病久了，胡乱投医；吃药过多，伤了元气。
一步错啦，步步错；时至今日，难以自我。
人的痛苦，也是一种幸福！苦的资源，要好好解读！
人的一生，为了感觉和理想；只要人活着，就有希望实现愿望！
从现在做起，从自己做起！休养生息，准备东山再起！
黎明之前，黑夜凄凉；无奈之中，盼望伯乐孙阳！
你越苦想，感觉时间越漫长；只有在创造之中，才能见到希望！

《一二三》

（9）身体差（042）

身体差，处处怕；拿不起，放不下。
小活力，大思想；常幻想，常惆怅。
能力小，想非非；到眼前，就心灰。
不如人，生嫉恨；不找错，灾乐祸。
为什么，不如人？其根本，在自身！
为什么，自身差？有原因，在爸妈！
感于头，实在身；官之病，胞是根。
人有病，难立身！国有病，难立尊！
防治病，先从根；人组国，国同人。
要授知，先授德！要治穷，先治病！

译文

身体素质差了，处处害怕；该拿的拿不起，该放的放不下。
小的活力，大的思想；经常幻想，经常惆怅。
能力小，想入非非；真到眼前，就心灰意冷啦。
不如别人，产生嫉妒恨；不找自己的错，有时又幸灾乐祸。
为什么，不如别人呢？其根本原因，在于自身因素！
为什么，自身差呢？有的原因，在于爸妈的遗传！
感觉在头上，实际在身上；器官的毛病，细胞是根源。
人有病啦，很难自理自立！国有病啦，很难树立尊严！
预防治疗疾病，要从根开始；人组成国家，国家如同个人一样。
要传授知识，先传授道德！要治疗贫穷，先治疗疾病！

第三章

（10）临危机（043）

临危机，处苦难；早知此，是否前？
昔日感，已不见；物没变，是己变。
基因变，精力散；这世界，不想看。
地有情，天有眼；人世间，最留恋！
几十年，转眼间；早或晚，去那边。
人死后，魂上天；身成灰，归自然！
找前人，到祠堂；无墓碑，植物旺。
兴祠堂，回故乡；叶归根，向天堂！
人间堂，如何上？求真正，美善创！
家族法，要真正；家族兴，天下明！

译文

面临危机，深处苦难；早知如此，是否还向以前那样做呢？
过去的感觉，已经不见啦；事物没有改变，是自己变啦。
基因变啦，精力散啦；这个世界，不想再看啦。
地是有感情的，天是有眼睛的；在人世间，是最舍不得离开的！
人的几十年，转眼之间；或早或晚地，都要去那边。
人死之后，灵魂上天；身体变成灰，回归自然！
寻找前面的人，需要去祠堂；没有墓碑，植物旺盛。
兴建祠堂，回到故乡；落叶归根，走向天堂！
人间天堂，如何去上？追求真正，完美善创！
家族的法规，需要客观公正；家族兴旺，天下文明！

《一二三》

（11）墙头草（044）

墙头草，随风倒；有森林，自然好。
能成树，谁愿草？能坐车，谁愿跑？
物天择，适生存；无基础，难上进。
怀大志，无力伸；无人理，无人问。
天不应，地不灵；难流泪，难感动。
人啊人！人啊人！谁知我，片苦心？
先天忧，后天乐；声声耳，事事心！
指江山，论英雄；我只想，把菜种。
草河边，望云飘；凌绝顶，众山小！
主沉浮，看今朝！谁真正，谁最好！

译文

墙头之草，随风而倒；有了森林，自然会好。
能变成树，谁愿变成草？能够坐车，谁愿在地上跑？
物竞天择，适者生存；没有基础，难以上进。
身怀大志，无力去做；无人搭理，无人询问。
叫天天不应，叫地地不灵；难以流泪，难以感动。
人啊人！人啊人！有谁知道，我的一片苦心呢？
先天下之忧而忧，后天下之乐而乐；声声入耳，事事关心！
指点江山，谈论英雄；我只想，去家里种菜谋生。
小草在河边，仰望云飘飘；若能凌绝顶，一览众山小！
谁主沉浮，还看今朝！谁能真正，谁就最好！

第三章

（12）临深溪（045）

临深溪，知地厚；登高山，知天高。
没有低，哪有高？没低潮，难高潮！
古雄才，多磨难；纨绔子，少伟男。
常恨铁，不成钢；多密植，少收粮。
毛换皮，换不及；马换羊，换不强。
捡芝麻，丢西瓜；常因小，而失大。
历苦难，才爱惜！经挫折，明事理！
失败得，最深刻！败交费，无所谓！
学历史，长经验；不听言，吃亏前。
不继往，难开来；不过渡，难加速！

译文

面临深溪，才知道大地很厚；登上高山，才知道天空很高。
没有低，哪来的高呢？没有低潮，也是难有高潮的！
自古雄才多磨难；纨绔子弟少伟男。
经常恨铁不成钢；过于密植少收粮。
鸡毛换蒜皮，越换越不及；五马换六羊，越换越不强。
捡了芝麻，丢了西瓜；经常因小而失大。
历经苦难，才知爱惜！经历挫折，才明白事理！
从失败中得到的，是最深刻的！因失败而缴费，无所谓！
学习历史，增长经验；不听老人言，吃亏在眼前。
不继承过去的，难以开创未来；不进行过渡，难于加速前进！

《一二三》

（13）哪里来（046）

哪里来？哪里去？哪些路？谁来陪？
妈妈生，到天堂！缤纷路，真善美！
人之初，是中性；善或恶，看谁领。
挨着勤，没有懒；你真正，他创善。
言传教，最有效；点点滴，如细雨。
讲事实，摆道理；谈谈心，论论理。
越打骂，越背离；难化解，逆心理。
常成惯，惯成然；然本性，难改变！
三看大，七看老；基础育，最重要！

译文

我从哪里来？要到哪里去？要走哪些路？路上谁来陪？
你是妈妈生，要到天堂去！五彩缤纷路，真正创善美！
人出生时，是中性；后来好或坏，要看怎么去领教。
挨着勤的，没有懒的；你真正了，他就会接着创善。
言传身教，是最有效果的；点点滴滴，如同细雨。
要讲事实，摆道理；要谈谈心，论论理。
你越打骂，越会背离正确；难以化解，逆反心理。
经常成习惯，习惯成自然；自然是一种本性，就很难改变啦！
三岁好坏，可知大了好坏，七岁怎样，就知一生怎样；基础教育，是最重要的！

（14）好教育（047）

好教育，在哪里？许多人，在寻觅。
千里马，在哪里？读《马说》，问韩愈。
八小时，工作日；孩学习，你说几？
从黎明，到深夜；缺午休，苦学习。
苦学生，像奴隶；超负荷，无兴趣。
字如米，业如山；脊柱弯，近视眼。
被累坏，谁去管？追其责，谁承担？
好教育，强身体！教做人，长能力！
琴棋书，德武体；无课程，怎学习？
教改革，最急需；望上下，共努力！

译文

好的教育，在哪里呢？有许多人，都在寻觅。
千里马，在哪里呢？阅读《马说》，询问韩愈。
八个小时，一个工作日；孩子的学习，你说几个小时？
从黎明，到深夜；缺乏午休，刻苦学习。
苦的学生，就像奴隶一样；超负荷工作，没有兴趣。
字如米小，业如山高；脊柱变弯了，变成近视眼了。
被累坏了，谁去管呢？追其责任，谁去承担？
好的教育，强健身体！教会做人，增长能力！
琴棋书画，德智武体；没有课程，怎么去学习？
教育改革，最为急需；希望上下，共同努力！

《一二三》

(15) 古英雄 (048)

古英雄，出少年；要成才，从小炼。
早起床，早睡眠；真正事，不间断。
盘中餐，粒粒苦；要节约，要朴素。
按趣好，定目标；近取材，步步高。
在家中，从父母！在学校，听师教！
自己事，自己办；门窗等，想开关。
炼能力，打苍蝇；飞动静，百发中。
有危险，快呼叫；想办法，赶快跑！
身干净，衣整齐；轻敲门，允进去。
说您好，明来意；多敬人，表谢意！

译文

自古英雄出少年；要想成才从小炼。
早些起床，早些睡眠；真正该做的事，要不间断地去做。
谁知盘中餐，粒粒皆辛苦；需要节约，需要朴素。
按照兴趣爱好，确定目标；就近取材，步步升高。
在家中，服从父母！在学校，听从师教！
自己的事，要自己办；门窗等，想着开和关。
锻炼能力，拍打苍蝇；飞的，动的，静止的，百发百中。
有危险时，赶快呼叫；想想办法，赶快逃跑！
身体干净，衣服整齐；轻轻敲门，允许之后再进去。
说您好，表明来意；要多尊敬人，最后表示谢意！

第三章

（16）行千里（049）

行千里，母担忧；父母事，放前头！
出家门，要谨慎；不沾光，慎助人。
有便宜，你要占；很可能，会受骗！
免费餐，不要吃；见钱物，不要拾。
防人心，不可无！害人心，不可有！
凭正心，去做事！心不亏，不怕鬼！
过路前，停一停；车较远，快通行。
在家穷，在路富；吃喝穿，钱备足！
夜行车，遇车人；换近光，是本分。
是好车，不挡道；是好人，不堵门！

译文

儿行千里母担忧，父母事情放前头！
出了家门，需要谨慎；不要沾光，谨慎助人。
如有便宜你要占；很有可能会受骗！
免费的饭，不要去吃；见到钱物，不要去拾。
防人之心不可无！害人之心不可有！
凭着正心去做事！心里不亏不怕鬼！
过马路之前，要停一停；车离较远，赶快通行。
在家里省，在路上富；把吃的喝的穿的和钱，准备充足！
夜里行车，遇到车和人；换成近光灯，是一种该做的本分。
如果是好车，就不要挡着道路；如果是好人，就不要堵人家的门！

《一二三》

（17）淡泊志（050）

淡泊志，宁静远；除歪恶，行正善。
知廉耻，懂礼仪；任何事，全无欺！
自己的，就争取；别人的，不惦记。
无伤害，求共赢；适可止，量力行。
合就换，不就散；不强求，不挽留。
退海空，让平和；吃亏福，舍就得。
缺德人，欺善软；正防卫，见勇为。
心要宽，力要大；拿得起，放得下！

译文

淡泊明志，宁静致远；除去歪恶，施行正善。
知道廉耻，懂的礼仪；任何事情，全无欺骗！
是自己的，就要争取；是别人的，不要惦记。
没有伤害，寻求共赢；适可而止，量力而行。
合适就交换，不合就离去；从不强求，从不挽留。
退一步海阔天空，让三分心平气和；吃亏是福，舍去就得。
缺德之人，欺负善软；要正当防卫，要见义勇为。
心胸要宽，力量要大；要拿得起，要放得下！

第三章

（18）人客气（051）

人客气，不当真；己客气，要用心。
别人好，不忘记；自己好，不要提。
思己过，不揭短；沉默金，笑少言。
病口入，祸口出；把口关，岁岁安！
要尊重，人隐私；不猜测，不传播。
黄赌毒，不靠近；一失足，千古恨！

译文

别人客气，不要当真；自己客气，要用真心。
别人的好，不要忘记；自己的好，不要去提。
想自己的过错，不要揭别人的短处；沉默是金，多笑少说。
病从口入，祸从口出；严把口关，岁岁平安！
要尊重别人的隐私；不去猜测，不去传播。
黄赌毒，不要靠近；一旦失足，就会变成，千古之恨！

《一二三》

（19）你有情（052）

你有情，我有谊；做事情，很容易。
常来往，久生情；不联系，变陌生。
多尊重，多鼓励；不埋怨，不打击。
好朋友，长相依；互相信，无秘密。
你助人，人助你！等价换，是天理！

译文

你有真情，我有友谊；共同做事情，就会很容易。
经常来往，日久生情；不再联系，变得陌生。
要多尊重，多鼓励；不要埋怨，更不要打击。
好的朋友，长期相依；互相信任，没有秘密。
你帮助别人，别人帮助你！等价交换，是客观真理！

第三章

（20）天下熙（053）

天下熙，为利来；天下攘，为利往。
花钱易，挣钱难；不细流，怎长远？
你理财，财理你；多用心，多收益。
有鸡蛋，多放篮；有钱物，放多处。
多转转，多看看；多家后，要果断。
让预交，不或少；以避免，中圈套！

译文

天下熙熙，皆为利来；天下攘攘，皆为利往。
花钱容易挣钱难；不细水长流，怎么能够长远？
你去理财，财就理你；多多用心，多多收益。
有了鸡蛋，要放在多个篮子里；有了钱物，要放在多个地方。
要多转转，要多看看；多家之后，要果断交换。
让你预交，不交或少交；以避免，中了别人的圈套！

《一二三》

(21) 人精神（054）

人精神，很重要；到医院，病就好。
平常时，心情好；一遇事，就烦恼。
快得失，受不了；警钟敲，要知道！
心有事，不愉快；说喊哭，放出来。
不出口，也可以；麻烦你，动动笔。
跑跑步，舒舒怀；爬爬山，看看海。
减负荷，强身体；好生活，属于你。
不在位，不谋政；人退休，心轻松！

译文

人的精神因素，是很重要的；有人到了医院，病就好啦。

平常的时候，心情很好；一遇到事，就烦恼。

马上得到或失去，心里受不了；这是警钟在敲，一定要知道！

心里有事情，不愉快；一定要通过说话，喊叫和痛哭等途径释放出来。

不通过口也可以；麻烦你动动笔写出来。

可以跑跑步，舒舒怀；也可以爬爬山，看看海。

减掉负荷，强健身体；好的生活，永远属于你。

不在其位，不谋其政；人退休之后，心里轻松！

第三章

（22）有活力（055）

有活力，感神奇；正感受，是目的。
力定感，思生梦；被尿憋，梦找坑。
动感好，最有能；思与梦，更多情。
思想好，身适中；在梦中，更轻松。
梦感好，身下行；思与动，难适应。
梦不行，身有病；快休养，慢慢行！
动思梦，力不同；大到小，要顺从。
看景色，不如听；听带想，看带行。
感觉好，信心大；啥事情，都不怕！

译文

有了活力，就会感到神奇；正确的感受，是人生的目的。

活力决定感觉，思想产生梦；睡觉中需要尿尿，有时候做梦就会寻找茅坑。

行动感觉好，最有能力；思想和做梦，会更好。

动感差，但是思想好，身体状况适中；在梦中，更加轻松。

只是梦感好，身体已经下行；思与动，难以适应。

连梦都不好，身体可能已经有病；需要尽快休养，做事慢行！

行动，思想和梦想，它们所需要的活力不同；依次从大到小，我们要顺从。

看景不如听景好；因为听景带着思想，看景带着行动。

感觉好啦，信心就大啦；不管做什么事情，都不害怕！

《一二三》

（23）粮油菜（056）

粮油菜，盐蛋奶；最解渴，温白开。
多吃菜，少吃粮；少吃盐，不吃糖。
细嚼咽，感香甜；基因健，活力现。
定量时，按正顺；0添加，菜养人。
少吃肉，不烟酒；常静养，常午休。
常变化，常调理；好养生，阴阳平。
多管下，对症药；姜汤条，治感冒。
合理活，是良药；要治病，靠睡觉！
命周期，二四半；正中医，最保健！

译文

必需品依次是，粮油菜和盐蛋奶；最能解渴的是，温白开水。
要多吃菜，少吃粮；要少吃盐，最好不要吃糖。
细嚼慢咽，感觉香甜；基因健康，活力出现。
定量定时，按照正确顺序；不添加化学物品，蔬菜养人。
少吃肉，不吸烟，不喝酒；经常静养，经常午休。
经常变化，经常调理；好的养生，阴阳平衡。
多管齐下，对症下药；带姜的热面条，可以治疗感冒。
合理生活，是最好的良药；要想治病，依靠睡觉！
生命周期是十二；正确的中医治疗，最能保护健康！

（24）养身体（057）

养身体，从小起；为安康，善待己。
人血糖，定活力；正常稳，最给力！
一器官，拖后腿；多系统，受连累。
薄弱环，要护好；统一调，靠大脑。
口嗓眼，若现干；内分泌，已缺短。
身放松，眼闭关；深呼吸，肢舒展。
口水多，泪出眼；健身功，告一段。
卧前后，坐一坐；流流泪，幸福多。
卧如弓，坐如钟；站如松，行如风！
中太极，印瑜伽；有同理，不同法。

译文

养护身体，要从小做起；为了安全健康，要好好对待自己。
人的血糖，决定人的活力；正常又稳定，是最给力的！
如果有一个器官拖了后腿；多个系统就会受到连累。
薄弱的环节要保护好；统一调节，依靠大脑。
口嗓眼，若出现干燥，说明内分泌已经短缺啦。
身体放松，眼睛闭上；深深地呼吸，四肢慢慢舒展。
口水多啦，眼泪出来啦；在做的健身功，可以告一段落啦。
躺卧之前之后，可以适当地静坐一下；流流眼泪，幸福多多。
躺卧如弓，坐如金钟；站如青松，行如疾风！
中国的太极拳，印度的瑜伽功；有同样的道理，不同的方法。

《一二三》

（25）关关鸠（058）

关关鸠，在河洲；窈窕女，君好逑。
绿草苍，白雾茫；有佳人，在水方。
好气质，纯净神；浓妆抹，已失真。
好男人，能力大；真正创，保国家。
好女人，温良俏；自立强，不唠叨。
男双因，易变心；女单因，最纯真。
己孩子，己最亲；人偶美，不动心。
志道合，互关心；爱越长，情越深！

译文

关关之鸠，在河之洲；窈窕淑女，君子好逑。
绿草苍苍，白雾茫茫；有位佳人，在水一方。
好的气质，清纯，干净，有精神；浓妆艳抹，已经失去了真实。
好的男人，能力巨大；真正地创造，保护国家。
好的女人，温和，善良，美丽；自立自强不唠叨。
男人双基因，容易变心；女人单基因，最纯真。
自己的孩子，自己最亲；别人配偶美，不要动心。
志同道合，互相关心；爱的越长，情谊越深！

(26) 君子交（059）

君子交，淡如水；如有事，尽力为。
小人交，不喝水；遇大事，各自飞。
树浇根，人交心；要学会，互感恩！
萝卜快，不洗泥；人饥渴，不挑剔。
人有难，去救急；人一生，不忘记。
路遥远，知马力；日长久，见人心！

译文

君子之交淡如水；如有事情尽力为。
小人之交不喝水；遇到大事各自飞。
浇树浇根，交人交心；要学会，互相感恩！
萝卜快了不洗泥；人饥渴了不挑剔。
别人有困难，自己去救急；别人一生，不会忘记。
路遥远，知马力；日长久，见人心！

《一二三》

（27）亲兄弟（060）

亲兄弟，明算账；糊涂账，和气伤。
要讲清，要说明；不能缺，正流程。
是亲戚，不犯财；弄不好，两不来。
九个好，一个坏；不记好，光记坏。
知人面，难知心；画龙虎，难画骨！
老牛儿，吃嫩草；老头儿，娶姑娘。
牛和草，是两样；老少人，各得想。
癞蛤蟆，想天鹅；真正创，有希望。
汉高祖，朱元璋；谁能想，能成皇？

译文

亲兄弟也要明算账；糊涂账会引起和气伤。
事先要讲清楚，说明白；不能缺正确的流程。
亲戚之间，最好不要来往钱财；弄不好双方都不高兴。
你对他九个好，一个坏；他可能不计你的好，广记着你的坏。
知人知面难知心；画龙画虎难画骨！
老牛喜欢吃嫩草；老头喜欢娶大姑娘。
牛和草之间差别很大；老头和姑娘都是人，他们各得其想。
癞蛤蟆想吃天鹅肉；如果真正地去创造，那是有希望的。
汉高祖刘邦，明朝的朱元璋；谁能想到，他们能成为皇帝呢？

（28）明知道（061）

明知道，这样错；为什么，不改过？
长期错，成习惯；改过来，不自然。
上船易，下船难；志不坚，难归还。
向下易，向上难；真不正，难创善。
悬崖马，回头岸；忍割爱，为长远。
药苦口，利于病；言逆耳，利于行。
他山石，可攻玉；远处僧，会念经！

译文

明明知道这样不对；为什么不改过来呢？
因为长期错，成了习惯；再改过来，感到不自然。
上船容易，下船难；志不坚强，难归还。
向下容易，向上难；客观不公正，难以创善。
悬崖勒马，回头是岸；忍痛割爱，为了长远。
良药苦口利于病；忠言逆耳利于行。
它山之石，可以攻玉；远处的和尚会念经！

《一二三》

（29）南辕辙（062）

南辕辙，方向错；何年月，到楚国？
狼小羊，自矛盾；假虎威，木三分。
掩耳铃，刻舟剑；郑人履，心不转。
守待兔，拔苗长；叶公龙，无希望。
农夫蛇，东郭狼；胸有竹，不莽撞。
马过河，亡羊牢；鸦喝水，不等靠。
古开天，公移山；龟兔赛，靠久专！

译文

南辕北辙，方向错了；何年何月，到达楚国？
狼和小羊，自相矛盾；狐假虎威，入木三分。
掩耳盗铃，刻舟求剑；郑人买履，心里不转。
守株待兔，拔苗助长；叶公好龙，没有希望。
农夫与蛇，东郭与狼；胸有成竹，不再莽撞。
小马过河，亡羊补牢；乌鸦喝水，从不等靠。
盘古开天，愚公移山；龟兔赛跑，龟靠久专！

第三章

（30）回头望（063）

回头望，我故乡；趣事多，在传说。
庵上女，是活头；高公庄，窝透气。
西小辛，东郭固；不小心，到郭固。
章华堡，藏弥寺；堡子城，老先生。
砸什么，不砸壶；淋什么，不淋车。
董吕庄，心不齐；未打井，两撇戏。
自挖井，孙武举；孙老河，娘娘戏。
仨黑的，俩白的；一菜花，在头里。
刘过继，写送据；明骗人，难说理！
说没有，送家里；庄上楼，任家的！

译文

回头仰望，我的故乡；趣事多多，在传说。
庵上闺女，头活动；高公庄的窝窝，上面透气。
西边的小辛村，东边的郭固村；因为不小心，嫁到郭固村。
章华堡，有个藏弥寺；堡子城，有个老先生。
砸什么也不能砸，我的壶；淋什么也不能淋，我的车。
董吕庄，心不齐；未曾打井，两撇子戏。
自己挖井的是，孙家武举人；孙老河，专唱娘娘戏。
仨黑地，俩白地，一个菜花在头里。
刘家过继，书写送的凭据；明明在骗人，难以说理！
说没有，夜里又给人送到家里；庄上的楼，是任家的！

《一二三》

（31）无心柳（064）

无心柳，柳成荫；谋在心，成在人。
打肿脸，充胖子；死要面，活受罪。
瑜打盖，打愿挨；人世间，谁悲哀？
井观天，郎自大；王别姬，死天涯。
前怕狼，后怕虎；得失后，是否悟？
踏破鞋，无觅处；水到成，水落出。
河没鱼，市上看；林越大，鸟越全。
螂捕蝉，雀在后；创善美，正无忧！

译文

无心插柳柳成荫；谋事在心，成事在人。
打肿脸充胖子；死要面子活受罪。
周瑜打黄盖，一个愿打，一个愿挨；人世之间谁悲哀？
坐井观天，夜郎自大；霸王别姬，死在天涯。
前面怕狼，后面怕虎；得失之后，是否领悟？
踏破铁鞋无觅处；水到渠成，水落石出。
河里没鱼市上看；树林越大，鸟儿越全。
螳螂捕蝉，黄雀在后；创造奉献美好，公正无忧！

（32）我家乡（065）

我家乡，干旱凉；好过去，在梦乡。
天和气，走下坡；好环境，在萎缩。
旱或淹，冷或热；哪里有，安乐窝？
特朗普，你他我！不作死，才能活！
大自然，无偏见；多中少，对等换。
地水多，天水淹；地越干，天越旱。
风雨顺，系统健；各环节，和相连。
假歪费，恶丑追；真正创，善美随！

译文

我的家乡，既干旱，又凄凉；好的过去在梦乡。
天气状况走下坡；好的环境在萎缩。
或旱或淹，或冷或热；哪里有安乐窝呢？
特朗普，你他我；不作死，才能活！
大自然是没有偏见的；多中少，对等交换。
地上水多，天上水淹；地上越干，天上越旱。
风调雨顺，系统健全；各个环节，和谐相连。
假歪费了，恶丑紧追；真正创了，善美紧随！

《一二三》

（33）互联网（066）

互联网，最美惑；好坏事，都能做。
用得好，创善美；用不好，人家毁。
玩手机，迷游戏；夜不睡，早不起。
身疲劳，心靡靡；误工作，误学习。
为未来，定法律；限网贷，限游戏。
控手机，好作息；正创善，人人喜。
好信仰，好目标；善用机，提前到。
自由行，靠平衡；自控行，靠真正。
中文化，手机网；真正创，善美望！

译文

互联网是最美，最具有诱惑力的；好事和坏事，都能去做。
用的好了，能够创造善美；用不好，个人和家庭，有可能被毁掉。
玩弄手机，迷恋游戏；夜里不睡，早晨不起。
身体疲劳，心情萎靡；耽误工作，耽误学习。
为了未来，要制定法律；限制网贷，限制游戏。
控制手机，好好作息；正确地去创造和奉献，人人喜欢你。
好的信仰，好的目标；善于用手机，可以提前到目标。
自由行，靠的是平衡；自控行，靠的是真正。
中国文化和手机网络；是真正创善美的希望！

第四章

《一二三》

（1）创善美（067）

没有真，哪有正？没有正，哪有创？
没有创，哪有善？没有善，哪有美？
没有美？歌颂谁？没有谁，真可悲？
万事物，守真正；人撇捺，双支撑。
说真话，难上难；正创善，怎实现？
说是是，不也是；没实事，何求是？
鹿为马，桑骂槐；人心坏，天下败！
不是云，难为水！只真正，创善美！

译文

没有真，哪里会有正？没有正，哪里会有创？
没有创，哪里会有善？没有善，哪里会有美？
没有美，我们歌颂谁？没有什么，我们真可悲？
万事物，遵守真正；人字一撇一捺，是双支撑。
说真话，难上加难；公正地创造奉献，怎么能够实现？
说是就是，不是也是；没有实事，如何求是？
指鹿为马，指桑骂槐；人心若坏，天下必败！
不是云，是难以成为雨水的！只有真正，才能创造善美！

（2）大学道（068）

大学道，在明德；在亲民，在至善。
知有定，定能静；静能安，安虑得。
有本末，有始终；知先后，则近道。
先格物，后致知；先意诚，后心正。
先修身，后齐家；再治国，平天下。
《大学》道，《中庸》观；真正创，善美念！
何为根？何为末？知因果，再想做！

译文

大学之道，在明明德；在亲民，在止于至善。
知止后有定，定而后能静；静而后能安，安能虑，虑能得。
物有本末，事由始终；知所先后，则近道矣。
先除私欲，后得真相；先心意真诚，后心念端正。
先修其身，后齐其家；然后再治国，平天下。
《大学》之道，《中庸》之观；是真正创善美的理念！
什么为根？什么为末？知道因果，再去想做！

《一二三》

（3）定时向（069）

定时向，看太阳；北极星，对南方。
人十指，十位制；地月期，定度时。
会看的，看门道；不会的，看热闹。
县官大，不现管；远水多，不解渴。
要受礼，不碰兵；吃半头，不吃整。
要公正，凭实力；明真实，需证据。
不真正，不彻底；后遗症，难处理！

译文

确定时间和方向，要看太阳；北极星对着南方。

人有十个手指，采用十进位制；地球月亮的周期，确定着圆度和时间。

会看的，就看门道；不会看的，就看热闹。

县官虽大，但不现管；远水虽多，但不解渴。

要接受礼待，不要碰硬的；要吃小亏，不吃大亏。

要想公正，全凭实力；要说明真实，需要证据。

如果不真正，不彻底；后遗症是难以处理的！

第四章

（4）多和少（070）

多和少，是需要；多就出，少就入。
不需要，不发展；不发展，不需要。
需发展，如鸡蛋；一代代，向下传。
同需要，必竞争；互补需，双方兴。
能定事，事靠能；互相需，成正比。
一定事，靠定能；要成功，超平衡！
想和做，互因果；需发展，靠想做！

译文

多和少，是两种需要；多了就会出，少了就会入。

不需要，就不发展；不发展，就不需要。

需要和发展，就像鸡和蛋一样；一代一代地向下传。

同样的需要，必然会竞争；互相补充的需要，就会双方兴旺。

能力决定事情，事情依靠能力；他们互相需要，成正比例。

一定的事情，依靠一定的能力；要想成功，能力最好超过这一平衡数值！

想和做，互为因果；需要和发展，靠的是想和做！

《一二三》

（5）丛林中（071）

丛林中，最野蛮；弱强食，无序展。
胜者王，败者寇；谁强大，谁霸权。
奉阴违，喊捉贼；比豺狼，心更黑。
借假歪，得恶费；自以为，非常美。
是歪心，惹的祸；怨月亮，是瞎说。
占着坑，最得利；干打雷，不下雨。
独一份，让人急；背离乡，去外地。
正创善，空悠悠；难流行，让人愁！
众亲离，向善美；若违背，必自毁！
天下鸦，一样黑；变天鹅，向上飞！

译文

丛林之中，是最野蛮的；弱肉强食，无序发展。
胜者为王，败者为寇；谁强大，谁会霸权。
阳奉阴违，贼喊捉贼；比豺狼，心更黑。
凭借假歪，得到，罪恶和浪费；自己认为还非常美。
是自己的歪心，惹的祸；埋怨月亮，纯粹是瞎说。
自己占着好位置，最能得利；广说好话，不办真事。
只有这一份，让人着急；没有别的办法，只有去外地。
公正，创造和奉献，空悠悠；难于流行，让人忧愁！
众叛亲离，走向善美；倘若违背，必然自毁！
天下乌鸦一样黑；变成天鹅向上飞！

（6）熊掌鱼（072）

熊掌鱼，二选一；要熊掌，不要鱼。
命财誉，做对比；先保命，再财誉。
刘文学，斗地主；两个人，谁更蠢？
正理智，强欲望；如何做，不受伤？
要学会，多变通；条条路，通北京！
俗随乡，市随行；变随机，心正良。
刚易断，柔易变；刚柔济，最美丽！
己不欲，他所欲；施于人，何不宜？

译文

熊掌和鱼，二者选其一；要熊掌，不要鱼。
生命，财产和名誉，做对比；先保命，然后是财产和名誉。
刘文学，斗地主；两个人，谁更愚蠢呢？
正的理智，强的欲望；如何去做，才能不受伤害？
要学会，多多变通；条条道路，通向北京！
俗要随乡，市要随行；变要随机，心要正良。
刚强易断，柔软易变；刚柔相济，最为美丽！
自己不需要，他人需要；给与他人，为何不适宜呢？

《一二三》

（7）物基础（073）

物基础，人上筑；物定人，人用物。
人资源，成衡比；计划育，万年计！
合理存，非常好；零储存，命难保。
进出差，定多少；正开节，多创造。
该出的，分不少！该进的，分分保！
要致富，多条路；优生育，爱植物！
要吃饭，家生饭；要穿衣，真纯棉。
肚清清，心明明；感美美，得长生！

译文

物体是基础，人是上层建筑；物体决定人，人利用物体。
人与资源，要成一定的平衡和比例；计划生育是万年大计！
合理的储存是非常好的；没有储存，生命难于保障。
进出之间的差，决定着储存的多少；要正确地开源节流，多些创造。
该付出的，一分也不少！该进入的，要分分保证！
要想致富，有多条之路；优生优育，爱护植物！
要想吃饭，家生便饭；要想穿衣，真的纯棉。
肚里清清，心里明明；感觉美美，得到长生！

（8）天经义（074）

天经义，月绕地；地绕阳，觉不像。
站地面，望日月；为什么，月残缺？
山雨来，风满楼；看一叶，能知秋。
看不清，听不懂；好距离，美朦胧。
有真正，有隐藏；为求知，听看想。
人需要，新奇鲜！越重复，越反感！
大世界，千万样；和合多，最兴旺。
仁者山，智者水；高山仰，正善美！

译文

天经地义的是，月亮环绕着地球；地球绕着太阳，感觉不像。
站在地面，仰望日月；为什么，月亮会出现残缺呢？
山雨欲来风满楼；看一片黄叶，能够知道秋天到了。
看不清，听不懂；好的距离，美的朦胧。
有真正，有隐藏；为了求知，才去听看想。
人需要，新的，与众不同的，鲜美的！越重复，越会反感！
大千世界，千种万样；和平，合作多，最为兴旺。
仁者爱山，智者爱水；高山敬仰，正善美！

《一二三》

（9）成萧何（075）

成萧何，败萧何；他垄断，人难活。
每个人，都随便；互碰撞，必混乱。
利一方，害一方；恶性环，如何管？
为自己，顾对方；管好己，爱多方。
多包容，多协商；平等让，路宽广。
分开做，正创多；次者让，优者上！
用他需，换我要；靠真正，去担保！
人为我，我为人！满人心，得万民！

译文

成也萧何，败也萧何；他垄断着，别人难以生活。
如果每个人，都随便；互相碰撞，必然混乱。
有利于一方，却又害另一方；出现恶性循环，如何去管理？
为了自己，要顾及对方；管好自己，爱护多方。
多多包容，多多协商；平等相让，道路宽广。
分开去做，正创会多；次者要让，优者要上！
用他需要的，换我需要的；依靠客观公正，去承担保证！
人人为我，我为人人；满足人民的心愿，就会得到大众的拥戴！

第四章

（10）有差异（076）

有差异，因物异；有底线，不能犯。
知缓急，定后先；按顺序，渐发展。
软中硬，直中间；快或慢，按需选。
不能轻，不能重；赏罚明，要适中。
有德能，多承担；常用物，在前面。
用真正，权利害；定现在，向未来！
利胜弊，助其生；弊胜利，控其命！

译文

如有差异，要因物而异；如对方有底线，就不要去犯。

先知缓急，后定后先；按照顺序，逐渐发展。

软中硬，直中间；快速或慢速等方法，要按需要去选择。

不能轻了，也不能重了；赏罚严明，要适中。

有道德和能力的人，要多承担些；经常用的物品，要放在前面的位置。

要用真正，权衡厉害；确定现在，面向未来！

利大于弊，要帮助其生长；弊大于利，要控制它的命脉！

《一二三》

（11）人方法（077）

人方法，是科技；是次序，加配比。
授人鱼，不如艺；得方法，创能力。
交换法，一对一；效最高，最简易。
良性争，是上计；有竞争，才进取。
弱对手，是下计；近得利，无长期。
助换方，是妙计；多交换，多受益。
同样话，不同说；会产生，不同果。
同样事，不同做；好方法，好结果。
各事物，喜温和；软着陆，收益多！
坏与好，皆比较；没最好，有更好！

译文

人的方法，就是科学技术；是做事的先后次序，加上原料配比。

给人物品，不如教会他如何得到物品的方法；得到了方法，就会创造能力。

一对一交换法；是效率最高，最简易的。

良性竞争，是好的方法；有了竞争，才会进取。

削弱对手，是不好的方法；近期得利，不会有长期利益。

帮助交换方，是很好的方法；多些交换，多些受益。

同样的话，不同的说法；会产生不同的结果。

同样的事，不同的做法；好的方法，会产生好的结果。

各种事物，喜欢温和；从慢到快逐渐交换，收益多多！

不好的和好的方法，都是比较而言的；没有最好，只有更好！

第四章

（12）人管理（078）

人管理，是能力；能力大，万事易。
身体好，感觉妙；活力旺，信心强。
有活力，生理想；找目标，找方向。
定标向，找途径；用方法，去行动。
找对象，去交换；能四素，力关键。
有目标，需规划；设计好，再方法。
能力到，商品换；其价值，必实现！

译文

人的管理，就是一种能力；能力大了，万事简易。
身体好了，感觉就会奇妙；体力脑力旺盛了，信心就会强。
有了活力，就会产生理想；然后寻找目标和方向。
确定目标方向后，就要寻找途径；然后运用好的方法去行动。
找到对象后，再去交换；能力的四要素，力量是关键。
有了目标，需要去规划；设计好了，再按一定的方法去做。
能力到了，商品交换这一步；它的价值，必然会实现！

《一二三》

（13）人做事（079）

人做事，如下棋；多观察，多分析。
正角度，美视听；全方位，要弄清。
听其言，观其行；人不正，事不共。
样样通，一样精；创奇迹，亿人用。
办大事，集大力；选用一，后备几。
要成功，多系统，各环节，密协同。
摆正位，各负责；正交换，共发展。
常检查，找隐患；正消除，保平安！
时刻备，创机会；时机到，正创美！

译文

人做事，如同下棋一样；需要多观察，多分析。
正确的角度，美好的视听；要从多方面，了解清楚。
要听其言，观其行；如果人不正，就不要同其共事。
样样了解，有一样精通；创造出特殊物品，亿人使用。
办大的事情，需要集中大的力量；选用一个，后面备用几个。
要想成功，需要多个系统；各个环节，密切协同。
摆正位置，各负其责；正确交换，共同发展。
时常检查，寻找隐患；正确消除，确保平安！
时刻准备，创造机会；时机到了，正确创造善美！

第四章

（14）人能力（080）

人能力，最重要！一切事，把它靠！
要认清，己粗长；按能力，定理想。
大就上，去开疆；小就让，去放羊。
做事前，想一想！做出后，会怎样？
有能力，全身心；伤人心，遭骂恨。
没条件，不去做；这才是，真负责！
关键时，要沉着；不知何，不去做！
用实据，去判断；正确后，要果敢！
一步天，一步位；事过度，定后悔！

译文

人的能力，是最重要的！一切的事情，都要把它依靠！
要认清，自己的实际情况；按照自己的能力，确定理想的大小。
能力大，就努力发展，开疆扩土；能力小，就退让，做些简单的事情。
做事之前，要想一想！做出之后，结果会怎么样？
有能力，就全力以赴地去做；否则，伤了人心，就会遭到骂恨。
没有条件，就不要去做；这才是真正的负责！
关键的时候，一定要沉着冷静；不知如何去做，就不要去做！
要用实际数据，去判断；正确之后，要果断勇敢！
一步登天，一步到位；做事过度，肯定后悔！

《一二三》

（15）有足能（081）

有足能，常任性；好结果，在手中。
人富足，好任性；多浪费，为高兴。
年轻人，时任性；碰钉后，慢慢通。
智能人，常深藏；做大事，如翻掌。
瓶不满，半摇晃；好张扬，躺中枪。
树越大，越招风；树欲止，风不停。
其原因，要弄清；不善改，择善从！

译文

有充足能力的人，经常任性；因为好的结果，把握在自己手中。
人富有的时候，喜欢任性；过多的浪费，为了高兴。
年轻人，有时会任性；遇到挫折之后，慢慢地就想通啦。
有智慧能力的人，时常深藏不露；做大的事情，易如反掌。
一瓶子不满，半瓶子摇晃的人；喜欢张扬，有时候躺着也会中枪。
树木越大，越会招风；树想不动，风却不停。
各种原因，要弄清；自己不好的要改掉，别人好的要学习利用！

第四章

（16）比能力（082）

比能力，不如你；比学历，高于你！
比效率，不如你；比关系，好于你！
比成绩，不如你；比资历，老于你！
无真正，心灰飞；创善美，无机会！
要发展，必改革；别光说，不去做！
说好听，不管用；关键是，看行动！
骡子马，遛遛看；用真正，去检验！

译文

比能力，不如你强；但是比学历，比你高！
比做事效率，不如你高；但是比同领导的关系，比你好！
比成绩不如你优秀；但是比资历，比你老！
没有客观公正，心灰人飞；创造善美，没有机会！
要想发展，必须改革；别光说，不去做！
光说好听的，是不管用的；关键要看行动怎么样！
是骡子是马，出来溜溜看就知道啦；要用真正去检验！

《一二三》

（17）各种事（083）

各种事，都有度；把好度，才成熟。
有看穿，不说穿；点到止，留尊面。
守真正，不过余；特情况，特办理！
人贵有，自知明；能力小，勿前行！
用鸡蛋，碰石头；既难看，又难受。
粘窝窝，太粘柔；粘到你，难脱手。
马蜂窝，要慎重；没把握，不要捅！

译文

做各种事情，都是有限度的；把好限度，你才会成熟。
有时候知道了，但不说出来；点到为止，有意给别人留下颜面。
遵守真正，不做过分的事；遇到特殊情况，要特殊办理！
人最可贵的是，知道自己的优缺点；经过比较，能力小，就不要去做！
用自己的鸡蛋，碰人家的石头；不仅难看，而且难受。
粘窝窝，太粘太柔；如果粘到你，是难以脱手的。
对于马蜂窝样式的情况，一定要慎重；没有绝对的把握，最好不要去捅！

第四章

（18）常对比（084）

常对比，知高低；知他人，知自己。
比人死，比货扔；若死扔，有何用？
身体差，要比下；知有余，得安息。
身体壮，要比上；知不足，去弥补。
找缺点，补缺陷；要吉祥，多扬长！
要定位，找参照；高大美，近目标。
好寻找，大到小；细微处，见分晓！

译文

经常对比，便知高低；了解他人，了解自己。
人比人就得死，货比货就得扔；如果死了或扔了，会有什么用呢？
身体差，就要同更差的比；知道比下有余，就能得到安全作息。
身体强壮，就要同更强的比；知道比上不足，就要去努力弥补。
寻找缺点，弥补缺陷；要想吉祥，多多发扬自己的长处！
要想确定位置，先寻找参照物；高大美的，接近目标的，就是参照物。
好的寻找，从大到小；细微之处，可见分晓！

《一二三》

（19）遇事情（085）

遇事情，不忙急；找原因，解问题。
知真正，知责利；站对方，去考虑。
事三端，互需要；勿封杀，多协调。
好沟通，当事层；若不成，向上行。
调解法，要推广；调解会，是桥梁。
宽待人，严律己；己管己，最彻底！

译文

遇到事情，不要着忙着急；要寻找原因，解决问题。

了解真相和正确途径，责任和利益；双方要站在对方的角度，去考虑问题。

事情的三方，互相需要；不能封杀，要多多协调。

好的沟通，要在当事双方；协调不成，再向上反映，进一步解决。

人民调解法，需要推广；调解委员会是当事双方的桥梁。

宽以待人，严于律己；自己管好自己，事情完美彻底！

（20）顾大局（086）

顾大局，舍小己；顾全面，抓重点。
处事道，中庸观；若极端，则必反。
人无路，偷骗抢；狗无路，急跳墙。
留余地，大家用！留后路，大家行！
话不满，事不完；里方正，外灵动。
道德宽，法律严；有规矩，才方圆。
凝共识，聚力量；为理想，真正创！

译文

要顾及大局，舍弃小的自己；要顾及全面，抓住重点。
好的处事之道，就是中庸的观点；如果做事极端，必然会走向反面。
人没办法的时候，可能会偷骗抢；狗没路的时候，可能会急着跳墙。
留下余地，大家共用！留下后路，大家共行！
话不说满，事不做完；心里公正，做事灵活机动。
道德要宽，法律要严；有了规矩，才成方圆。
凝合共识，聚集力量；为了理想，真正去创！

《一二三》

（21）在领导（087）

先射马，先擒王；为什么，要这样？
好不好，在领导！在团队！在换方！
好领导，带头上；常监管，指正向。
好团队，真正强；随应变，创无疆。
有交换，像弹簧；强就弱，弱就强。
有捷径，懒人创；为省事，变勤忙。
春江水，鸭先知；要创善，靠一线！
闭门车，难适合；强人坐，怨恨多。
求相同，存差异；按真需，去设计。
经思考，再计校；后制造，满需要！

译文

射人先射马，擒贼先擒王；为什么，要这样做呢？
因为好不好，在于领导！在于团队！在于与之交换的一方！
好的领导，要带头去做；经常监督和管理，指引正确的方向。
好的团队，真正地强大；能够随机应变，创造无限的疆土。
有的交换，就像弹簧一样；你强它就弱，你弱它就强。
有的捷径是懒人创造的；为了以后省事，现在变的非常勤忙。
春江水暖鸭先知；要想创善，必须依靠一线的人去做！
闭门造车，难以适合；强让别人去坐，怨恨会很多。
求相同，存差异；按照真正地需要，进行设计。
经过思考之后，再次进行设计校正；最后制造，满足需要！

第四章

（22）靠自己（088）

人独立，靠距离；自个体，勿过密。
把人靠，要回报；不救穷，难救急。
指正道，靠真理；理立强，靠自己！
靠自己，最便宜；靠自己，最彻底！
要成功，定目标；多积累，步步高。
知己彼，定具体；正选择，步步起。
顺天地，借众力；随机变，事专一。
好时机，快交易；互满足，共受益。
旦夕福，不测云；万年船，靠正心！

译文

人要独立，要靠距离；自己是单独个体，与他人不要过于亲密。
把人依靠，需要回报；不能救穷，难以救急。
指引正道，依靠真理；自理自立自强，要靠自己！
靠自己，是最便宜的；靠自己，是最彻底的！
要想成功，先确定目标；多多积累，步步升高。
知己知彼，确定具体；正确选择，步步做起。
顺应天地规律，借助众力；随机应变，做事专一。
好的时机，赶快交易；互相满足，共同受益。
人有旦夕祸福，天有不测风云；万年之船，靠的是一颗正心！

《一二三》

（23）为初心（089）

为初心，意志强；经常做，经常想。
人睡觉，我醒早；按计划，不等靠。
人花落，我未开；用点点，创未来。
人一天，我一年；用一生，去实现。
日积累，慢攀登；登峰极，炉火青。
不在高，有仙名！不在深，有龙灵！
不飞已，飞冲天！不鸣已，鸣惊人！

译文

为了初心，意志坚强；经常去做，经常去想。
别人睡觉，我要醒早；按照计划，不等不靠。
别人花落，我还未开；要用点点，创造未来。
别人一天，我用一年；要用一生，进行实现。
日积月累，慢慢攀登；登峰造极，炉火纯青。
山不在高，有仙则名！水不在深，有龙则灵！
不飞则已，一飞冲天！不鸣则已，一鸣惊人！

第四章

（24）争口气（090）

没人理，一条虫；虫变龙，万人迎。
鸡在叫，鸟在笑；鸡变凤，百鸟颂。
有什么，别有病！没什么，别没能！
有力量，有希望；真正强，善美扬！
为家国，为自己；光宗祖，荣归里。
争口气，争柱香；要自强，要向上。
尽我力，连天地；做自己，该做的。
不想帅，非好兵；身子正，不怕影。
未成功，需努力！龙传人，争第一！

译文

没人理会，一条虫；虫变巨龙，万人迎。
公鸡在叫，鸟儿在笑；鸡变凤凰，百鸟颂扬。
有什么，也别有病！没什么，也别没能！
有了力量，就有希望；真正强大了，要把善美发扬！
为了家国，为了自己；光宗耀祖，荣归故里。
人争一口气，佛争一柱香；我要自强，我要向上。
尽我之力，连接天地；要做自己该做的事情。
不想当元帅的士兵，就不是好士兵；身正不怕影子歪。
革命尚未成功，同志仍需努力；龙的传人，要争做第一！

《一二三》

（25）有的人（091）

有的人，心单纯；直来去，不做戏。
有的人，爱权利；耍心机，用其极。
潜规则，真是牛：挂羊头，卖狗肉。
双标准，真气人：不管己，管他人。
官管理，商贸易；官商勾，假歪臭。
上不正，下梁歪；小和尚，把经坏。
皇不急，太监急；太监急，无权力！
想美满，真骨感；要实现，一二三！

译文

有的人，心里单纯；直来直去，从不做戏。
有的人，热爱权利；玩弄心机，达到极端。
潜规则，真是牛啊：挂着羊头，卖着狗肉。
双标准，真气人啊：不管自己，专管他人。
官员做管理，商人做贸易；官商勾，假歪臭。
上梁不正，下梁歪；小和尚，把经给念坏。
皇上不急，太监急；太监着急，没权利！
理想是美满的，现实是骨感的；要想实现，需要三步走！

第四章

(26) 我恨你 (092)

咸丰帝,我恨你!为什么,要割地?
袁世凯,我恨你!为什么,要复辟?
蒋介石,我恨你!为什么,缺正义?
有的人,我恨你!为什么,背规律?
无真正,缺善创;自悲伤,后遭殃。
大趋势,谁能抵?九个九,终归一!
极感性,中理性;正创善,最英雄!
何来爱?何来恨?善得爱!恶得恨!

译文

咸丰帝,我恨你!你为什么,要割让外东北的土地?
袁世凯,我恨你!你为什么,要复辟帝制?
蒋介石,我恨你!你为什么,缺乏正义?
有的人,我恨你!你为什么,违背规律?
没有真正,缺乏善创;自己悲伤,后代遭殃。
大的趋势,谁能抵挡?即使是九个九,最终也得归为一!
极端感性,中端理性;正创善的人,是最英雄的人!
哪里来的爱?哪里来的恨?善良得到爱!罪恶得到恨!

《一二三》

（27）天无欲（093）

天无欲，自然刚；人无欲，去何方？
有欲望，有理想；真正换，如愿偿。
为悦容，为知死；为财死，为食亡。
打也来，骂也往；没好处，谁早床？
正私心，应发扬；方法当，应护航。
让付出，先得到；让奉献，先自保！
菩过河，自难保；靠什么，去行好？

译文

天是没有欲望的，自然就会刚强；人如果没有欲望，他去什么地方呢？

有了欲望，就有了理想；真正地交换，就会如愿以偿。

女为悦己者容，士为知己者死；人为财死，鸟为食亡。

打你也来，骂你也去；没有好处，谁会早早起床？

正当的私心，应该发扬去做；方法得当，国家应该护航。

让我付出，先要得到；让我奉献，先得自保！

泥菩萨过河，自身难保；依靠什么，去行好？

第四章

（28）权是力（094）

权是力，是管理；有好处，必付出。
责利绑，民监督；靠竞争，选举出。
公权力，重于山；要管好，必分权。
人人权，个个管；高效率，洪福天。
该不管，不该管；一管死，不管乱。
我权力，大家给；必真正，创善美！
为人民，无怨悔；对天誓，心无愧！
先自由，先去做；后管理，后改革。
改革法，应立项！监管法，应推广！
德法传，要到位！打官司，要免费！

译文

权是一种力量，是一种管理；有权有好处，但又必须付出。

对于掌权者，责任利益要捆绑，人民要监督；先靠竞争，后靠选举而出。

公共权力，重于泰山；要想管好，必须分权。

人人有权，个个管理；提高效率，洪福齐天。

该管的不管，不该管的管；一管就死，不管就乱。

我的权利，是大家给的；必须做到，真正创善美。

为了人民，无怨无悔；对天发誓，心中无愧！

首先自由，首先去做；然后发现问题，再去管理，再去改革。

改革法，应该立项！监管法，应该推广！

对道德法律的宣传，应该到位；各种打官司，需要免费办理！

《一二三》

（29）好人才（095）

好人才，能力全；识时务，通机变。
无人才，难发展；创业难，守更难。
用不疑，疑不用；定监理，是正行！
可上下，可曲张；察秋毫，知动向。
一了解，二计算，三方案，四实现。
要高效，小快早；处女地，正善造！

译文

好的人才，能力要全面；要认清形势，精通机变。

没有人才，难以发展；创业难，守业更难。

用人不疑，疑人不用；定期地监督管理，是正确的行动！

好人才可上可下，可曲可张；能够察觉事物丝毫的变化，知其发展动向。

一能了解情况，二能归纳计算；三能提出行动方案，四能具体实现。

要想高效，需要小型、快速、提前；在没有别人做的地方，正确地奉献和创造！

第四章

（30）奔统一（096）

先私有，吃穿住；后家富，安康福。
先真正，立德法；后创善，美国家。
主人公，最自豪！愿负责，勇创造！
尽才用，按劳配；顾弱势，好社会。
一二三，步步宽；云中步，日中天。
周共和，秦统一；民国去，中国立。
同心德，力合一；兴中华，奔统一！

译文

首先要个人拥有，才能够吃穿住；然后家里富裕啦，才能够安康福。

首先要客观公正，才能够立德法；然后创造奉献啦，才能够美好国家。

主人公，是最自豪的！愿意负责，勇于创造！

人尽其才，物尽其用，按劳分配；顾及弱势群体，是好的社会。

一二三，一步比一步更宽；云中漫步，如日中天。

从周朝的共和，到秦朝的统一；从中华民国的离去，到中华人民共和国的建立。

同心同德，力量合一；振兴中华，奔向统一！

《一二三》

(31) 买租借 (097)

买租借,要分清;按实情,做决定。
有闲钱,不买闲;钱生钱,最合算。
有条件,又常用;选购买,心轻松。
有没有,用不用;选租用,最中庸。
易进出,无人情;无折旧,心平衡。
借人物,靠人情;没关系,宁不用。
不得已,去借用;多爱护,早归送。
如万一,出事情;真心赔,多沟通!

译文

对于买租借三种情况,要分清楚;要按照实际情况,去做决定。

有了闲钱,不买没用的东西;用钱去赚钱,是最合算的。

有条件买,又经常使用;选择购买,心里轻松。

不管有没有条件,常用不常用;选择租用,是最适中的。

容易进出,又无人情;没有折旧,心里平衡。

借人家的东西,靠的是人情;没有那种人情关系,宁可不用,也不去借。

实在没有办法,去借用;要多加爱护,早早归送。

如果万一,出了事情;要真心去陪,多多沟通!

第四章

（32）众心理（098）

众心理，真奇怪；贱不买，贵不卖。
明商人，多心计；贵时卖，贱时积。
所有事，需时机；无好机，难受益。
学圣贤，楚范蠡；多方面，创奇迹！
中国人，靠农地；常保守，不进取。
犹太人，颠流离；靠生意，富无比。
重工贸，英法西；其文化，遍天地！

译文

大众的心理，真是奇怪；越贱越不买，越贵越不卖。
聪明的商人，有很多计谋；贵的时候就卖，贱的时候就买货积累。
所有的事情，都需要时机；没有好的时机，是难以得到好处的。
要学习圣贤，楚国的范蠡；在多个方面，创造了奇迹！
中国人，过去依靠农业和土地；经常保守，不思进取。
犹太人，以前颠簸流离；依靠生意，富的无比。
重视工业和贸易的，英国，法国和西班牙；他们的文化，遍布天下！

《一二三》

（33）千里行（099）

千里行，始足下；事发展，潜默化。
要吃饭，口口吃；要说话，字字说。
要做事，小事起；一点点，大事易。
要管理，源头起；分类做，简又易。
水专久，滴石穿；人专久，能移山。
《今日诗》，今日做；《明日歌》，成蹉跎。
夜越长，梦越多；时机熟，不能拖！
今天事，做到位！明天事，今天备！

译文

千里之行，始于足下；事情的发展，潜移默化。
要想吃饭，就要一口一口地吃；要想说话，就要一字一字地说。
要想做事，从小事做起；一点一点地，大的事情就会变得容易。
要想管理，从源头做起；分类去做，简单又容易。
水专久了，能够把石头滴穿；人专久了，能够移动大山。
《今日诗》，说的是今天就做；《明日歌》，说的是明天再做。
夜里越长，做的梦越多；时机成熟了，不能拖延，必须赶快做！
今天的事，要做好！明天的事，今天做好准备！

第四章

（34）好信誉（100）

好信誉，是块宝；谁得到，谁就好。
先想好，再去说！言必行，行必果！
君一言，马难追；诺千金，从不悔。
有急事，做不了；想办法，提前告。
受人托，忠人事；没把握，不应诺。
言无信，是骗人；无人理，难生存。
说谎言，必善意；不伤人，护自己。
好借还，再不难；借不给，没下回！

译文

好的信誉，是块宝；谁得到了，谁就好。
先想好了，再去说；说了必做，做了必有成果！
君子一言，驷马难追；一诺千金，从不后悔。
万一有急事，做不了了；要想办法，提前告知。
受人之托，忠人之事；没有把握，不要应诺。
说话不算数，就是骗人；以后无人理会，难以生存。
说假话，必须是善意的；为了不伤害别人，为了保护自己。
好借好还，再借不难；借了不给，没有下回！

《一二三》

（35）为得到（101）

为得到，无私献；得到后，就变脸。
无真正，假歪遍；无创善，费恶现。
为享乐，缺监管；各自政，权利战。
家富兴，难三代；国寿命，难三百。
接力赛，靠人才；真正创，善美在。
探头下，谁违法？好监管，好天下！
十次故，九次快；稳中胜，步步来！

译文

为了得到，无私地去奉献；得到之后，就变了脸。
没有真正，假歪普遍；没有创善，费恶出现。
为了享乐，有意缺乏监管；各自为政，大打权利战。
家庭富兴，难有三代；国家寿命，难有三百。
接力赛，靠的是人才；真正地去创造，善美才会常在。
探头之下，谁敢违法？好的监管，好的天下！
十次事故，九次快；稳中求胜，步步来！

第四章

(36) 路两条 (102)

路两条,不能少;进和退,要想好。
怎样去,何时地?怎样退,少吃亏?
先算坏,后算美!无胜算,韬光晦!
强就攻,中就守;弱就退,无就走。
城有人,好做官;能人钱,事条件。
铁公鸡,毛不拔;办事情,磨断爪。
有余粮,心不慌;艺高多,创富乐。
积善德,圣心备;积真正,创善美!

译文

道路有两条,是不能少的;进路和退路,都要想好。
怎样去,在何时何地?怎样退,才能少吃亏?
先算坏处,后算好处!不能必胜,就要韬光养晦!
强大就进攻,适中就防守;弱势就退让,无力就离走。
城里有人,好做官;有能力,有人脉,有资金,是做事的基本条件。
如果像铁公鸡一样,一毛不拔;办事情,就会非常困难。
家有余粮,心中不慌;武艺高多,创造富乐。
积善成德,圣心备矣;积累真正,创造善美!

《一二三》

（37）人吃穿（103）

人吃穿，最需要；没植物，何温饱？
人安康，最重要；若无皮，哪有毛？
真正创，最该要；没有果，如何消？
无需要，无利害；善美果，何处来？
上管理，中工艺；下生意，底种地。
天下人，最低高；没有民，谁能好？
真正人，要思考：怎样做，都能好？

译文

人的吃穿，是最需要的；如果没有植物，怎样温饱？

人的安康，是最重要的；如果没有皮了，哪里会有毛？

真正地创造，是最应该做的；没有创造的成果，怎样去消费？

没有需要，就没有好处和坏处；善美的结果，从哪里来呢？

上面是管理者，中间是加工手艺人；下面是做生意的，最底层是种地的。

天下的人，是最低和最高的；没有平民百姓，又有谁能够好呢？

真正的人，是需要思考的；怎样去做，大家都能好！

第四章

（38）一条河（104）

一条河，长深宽；源博深，水流远。
汛期时，不泛滥；干旱时，水不断。
一个人，好遗传；根本坚，能高攀。
少年学，真正善；成年后，创高远。
得机遇，必挑战；好或坏，能比言。
好多磨，来不易；需感受，需努力。
适外物，外适己；互相适，最得力！
历风雨，见彩虹；福如水，寿比松！

译文

一条河流，长深宽；水源博深，水流远。
汛期的时候，不泛滥成灾；干旱的时候，水流不断。
一个人，有好的遗传；根本坚固，能够高攀。
少年学习，真正善；成年之后，创高远。
要得机遇，必去挑战；好或者坏，是能力相比较而说的。
好事多磨，来之不易；需要感受，需要努力。
适应外物，外物适应自己；互相适应，是最能得到力量的！
历经风雨，见到彩虹；福如东海长流水，寿比南山不老松！

《一二三》

（39）一只掌（105）

一只掌，拍不响；双方责，不一样。
该低头，不挺仰；水低海，人低王。
给人便，给己便；互谅解，向前看。
进守退，性三面；中和换，路最宽！
双抗战，双伤残；鹬蚌争，渔翁赚。
狭路逢，智勇胜；高境界，变友朋。
水来屯，兵来挡；能化解，最正当。
保和平，正方强；魔高尺，道高丈。
要发展，靠供求；互补换，最长久！
远亲戚，不如邻；邻友善，最开心！

译文

一只手掌，是拍不响的；双方的责任，是不一样的。
该低头的时候，不要挺仰；水低为海，人低为王。
给别人方便，别人就给自己方便；要互相理解，向前看。
进攻，防守和撤退，性质三方面；中和性的交换，道路是最宽的！
双方抗战，双方伤残；鹬蚌相争，渔翁得利。
狭路相逢，智勇者胜；境界高了，变为朋友。
水来土屯，兵来将挡；能够化解，最为正当。
保护和平，正方要强；魔高一尺，道高一丈。
要想发展，依靠供求；互补交换，最为长久！
远方亲戚，不如邻居；与邻友善，最为开心！

第四章

（40）可不可（106）

可不可？比再说！质变量，定结果！
能达到，或超过；按计划，可以做。
达不到，小很多；好不要，尝苦果。
机成熟，快收割；实定行，不贪多。
不成熟，勿心急；找原因，多努力。
早机多，晚机少！不赶晚，要赶早！
掌主权，最美好！能调人，不被调！
无不能，无全能；有不为，为必胜！

译文

事情可不可做？先比较一下再说！进行质变的量，决定结果！
自己能达到，或者超过了那个量；按照计划，是可以做的。
自己达不到，或者小很多；最好不要，去尝苦果。
时机成熟，赶快收割；实际能力决定自己的行动程度，不要贪多。
时机不成熟，不要心急；寻找原因，多多努力。
早了机会多，晚了机会少！不要赶晚，要赶早！
掌握主动权，是最美好的！能调动别人，不被别人调动！
没有不能做的事，也没有全能做的事；有时候不做，只要做必定胜利！

《一二三》

（41）爱劳动（107）

爱劳动，人人敬；爱劳动，最光荣。
穷则变，变则通；要变通，靠劳动。
要生产，先劳动；得到后，才能用。
消费后，要长能；靠能力，感人生。
把能力，变劳动；创善美，最神圣。
劳动中，献热情；感轻松，最美幸。
要打铁，自身硬；让人做，先自行！
不随东，累无功；若不正，决不行！
君爱财，取有道；不正换，决不要！
劳一天，一夜安；劳一生，永安宁！

译文

热爱劳动，人人尊敬；热爱劳动，最光荣。
穷了就要变，变了就会通；要想变通，依靠劳动。
要向生产，先要劳动；得到之后，才能使用。
消费之后，要增长能力；依靠能力，感受人生。
再把能力，变成劳动；创造善美，最神圣。
劳动之中，奉献热情；感觉轻松，最美幸。
要想打铁，自身硬；让人去做，先自行！
干活不随东，累死也无功；如果不正确，决不去做！
君子爱财，取之有道；如果不是正确交换得到的，坚决不要！
劳动一天，一夜心安；勤劳一生，永得安宁！

第四章

（42）供供供（108）

供需差，定市场；谁市场，谁兴旺。
供大需，需市场；需大供，供市场。
供需平，互利赢；国泰安，人寿丰。
报价格，问又看；后交换，少麻烦。
随行进，随行出；成或败，信做主。
清白账，糊涂局；同档次，无差距。
质价应，系统善；大流通，赚大钱。
无对有，有对优；全都有，可转走。
市无情，人有情；按需要，去正行。
好计划，需市场；正理论，应上场！

译文

供需之差，决定市场；谁的市场，谁就兴旺。
供大于需，需方市场；需大于供，供方市场。
供需平衡，互利共赢；国泰民安，人寿年丰。
卖方报价格，买方问又看；然后交换，减少麻烦。
随着行情进，随着行情出；成功或失败，信誉在做主。
清白算账，糊涂结局；同样档次，没有差距。
质量价格适应，系统完善；大的流通，能赚大钱。
他无对我有，他有对我优；全都有了，可以考虑改行转走。
市场无情，人有情；按照需要，去正行。
好的公有计划，需要市场经济去完成；正确的理论，应该上场推行！

《一二三》

（43）小九九（109）

小九九，小打算；家家经，不好念。
一爱二，二爱三；互补爱，金难换。
老爱小，低爱高；对极交，妙不妙？
要无限，就聚变！要最好，就超导！
任鸟飞，凭鱼跳；各得所，人最好！
安乐窝，无限好；睡一觉，迎日照！

译文

小算计，小目标；家家有本，难念的经。

一喜欢二，二喜欢三；能够互相补充的爱，用金子也难以换来。

年老的喜欢年小的，低处的喜欢高处的；对称极端的交换，美妙不美妙呢？

要想无限，就要聚变！要想最好，就要超导！

天高任鸟飞，海阔凭鱼跳；各得其所，人类最好！

安乐窝，是无限好的；睡一觉，迎接日照！

第四章

（44）万事兴（110）

天时地，不如和；家中和，万事兴！
能力小，换错位；有差错，和为贵！
人多靠，龙多闹；统管行，到目标！
人同心，利断金；人同力，泰山移。
人组家，家组国；人人创，家国旺。
一枝秀，不是春；万花放，最迷人。
厚积累，薄进发；正信善，赢天下！

译文

天时地利，不如人和；家中和，万事兴！
因为能力小，没有把事情办好；有了差错，要以和为贵！
人多会靠，龙多会闹；进行统一管理和行动，就能到达目标！
人同心，其利断金；人同力，泰山可移。
个人组成家庭，家庭组成国家；人人创造，家国旺盛。
一枝独秀，不是春；万花齐放，最迷人。
厚厚积累，适当进发；依靠正确，诚信，善行，赢得天下！

第五章

《一二三》

（1）一个人（111）

一个人，一条路；每个人，不重复。
三顿饭，一身衣；一张床，一块地。
身外物，不过求；不带来，不带走。
笑一笑，十年少；愁一愁，白了头。
老保守，又小气；老来难，不容易。
外表美，像鲜花；真善美，才是家！
你有钱，怎么花？做慈善，乃最佳！
趁世界，属于你；献爱心，多努力！

译文

一个人，走一条路；每个人，都不会重复。
一天吃三顿饭，穿一身衣；睡一张床，占一块地。
身外之物，不要过于追求；生不带来，死不带走。
笑一笑，十年少；愁一愁，白了头。
人老了，保守又小气；老来难，做事不容易。
外表美，就像鲜花一样；真善美，才是你的家！
你有了钱，该怎么花呢？做慈善，是最好的！
趁这世界，还属于你；奉献爱心，要多努力！

（2）三目标（112）

三目标，活业情；人感觉，万万种。
满负荷，感最好；缺或超，最糟糕。
需香甜，不臭苦；人无用，如粪土。
想要好，常需要；想乐福，需满足。
光阴箭，日月梭；时金贵，不待我。
有心愿，快去做；转眼间，就老了。
正当时，交接班；需要时，多帮点。
出来混，总要还；主动福，被动患！

译文

三个目标，生活、事业和爱情；人的感觉，有万万种。

满负荷，感觉最好；缺负荷或者超负荷，都是最不好的。

需要就香甜，不需要就臭苦；人没有用了，就如同粪土一样。

想要得到好，就要经常需要；想要得到快乐和幸福，就让需要得到满足。

光阴似箭，日月如梭；时间金贵，不会等待我。

你有心愿，就赶快去做；转眼之间，你就老了。

合适的时候，你就交接班；需要你的时候，就来多帮点。

出来混，总是要还的；主动去还就是福，被动去还就是祸患！

《一二三》

（3）谋万世（113）

谋万世，谋全局；运帷幄，决万里。
谋好己，再谋远；小不正，大谋乱。
太自私，太眼前；高大远，难实现。
上有天，下有地；中间有，我自己。
要做事，先做人！正做人，真做事！
天地良，对得起！祖先孙，记心里！
假歪费，要抛弃！真正创，要尽力！

译文

谋划万世，谋划全局；运筹帷幄，决胜万里。
先谋好自己，再谋远处；小不正，则大谋乱。
如果太自私，太眼前；高大远的目标，是难以实现的。
上面有天，下面有地；中间有，我自己。
要想做事，先要做人！堂堂正正做人，认认真真做事！
天地良心，要对得起！祖先和子孙，要记心里！
假歪费恶，要彻底抛弃！真正创善，要尽力去做！

（4）怎么走（114）

人活着，怎么走？一二三，步步求。
不如意，怎么办？想办法，去改变！
进无力，退无地；固根基，多寻觅。
低调人，中调事；顺善养，逆忍创。
冷与热，都可怕；极端处，不安家。
上赚下，高管低；能力大，向上去！
身安健，多历练；找创机，和平换。
好了疤，忘了痛；不忍控，怎正行？
管住心，迈开腿！学真正，创善美！

译文

人活着，怎么走呢？一步两步三步，一步一步地去追求。
活着不如意，怎么办呢？要想办法，去改变！
前进没力量，后退没地方；要巩固根基，多多寻觅。
低调做人，中调做事；顺境善养，逆境忍创。
过冷与过热，都是可怕的；在极端之处，不要安家。
上面赚下面的，高处管低处的；如果能力大，要向上走！
身体安全健康，要多历练；寻找创造时机，要和平地同对方交换。
好了疤瘌，忘了痛；不忍控，怎么能够正确地行动呢？
要管住自己的心，迈开自己的腿；学习真正，创造善美！

《一二三》

（5）想成名（115）

想成名，先真正；得美名，必创奉！
学工蜂，采花蜜；学股神，把时机。
让人找，变成宝；综合工，满需要。
价格低，质量好；服务到，信誉高。
创善美，引人目；为人民，多服务！
你优秀，人找你；人优秀，找不易。
婆卖瓜，自己夸；真正好，谁人傻？
是金子，要发光；学毛遂，勇担当！

译文

想要成名，先要真正；得想美名，必须创奉！
学习工蜂，采花酿蜜；学习股神，把握时机。
让人寻找，先变成宝；综合加工，满足需要。
价格较低，质量较好；服务到位，信誉很高。
创造善美，引人注目；为了人民，多些服务！
你若优秀，别人找你；别人优秀；想找不易。
阿婆卖瓜，自己常夸；你若真好，谁人会傻？
若是金子，就要发光；学习毛遂，勇于担当！

（6）有信仰（116）

有信仰，不迷茫；好信仰，真正创。
真正追，不后悔；最好追，创善美。
最高界，是尊严；得尊严，生无憾。
先真正，后尊严；美尊严，必创善！
春蚕死，丝方尽；蜡成灰，泪始干。
港双平，王永庆；包玉刚，霍英东。
天乐校，逸夫楼；曹德旺，美千秋！

译文

有了信仰，不会迷茫；好的信仰，真正去创。
真正追求，不会后悔；最好追求，创造善美。
最高境界，就是尊严；得到尊严，一生无憾。
先有真正，后得尊严；完美尊严，必须创善！
春蚕到死，丝方尽；蜡炬成灰，泪始干。
香港庄世平，徐增平，台湾王永庆；包玉刚，霍英东。
古天乐学校，邵逸夫教学楼；首善曹德旺，他们爱中华，美千秋！

《一二三》

（7）多极化（117）

多级化，是规律；人群分，物类聚。
搞平衡，也可以；从根本，解问题。
产生因，是能力；同能力，差无几。
能之根，在身体；在真正，在机遇。
低学高，高帮低；人生观，向上提。
人价值，有大小；重泰山，轻鸿毛！
雁留声，人留名；正创善，照汗青！

译文

多极分化，是条规律；人会群分，物会类聚。
要搞平衡，那也可以；要从根本，解决问题。
产生原因，就是能力；同等能力，相差无几。
能力根本，就在身体；在于真正，在于机遇。
低要学高，高要帮低；人生观念，要向上提。
人生价值，有大有小；或重于泰山，或轻于鸿毛！
雁过留声，人过留名；正确创善，映照史册！

（8）有好钢（118）

有好钢，放刃上；有好粉，涂脸上。
有吃穿，奔安康；有真正，善美创。
数十年，转眼去；留什么，给这里？
别光说，我爱你！真善美，在哪里？
夕阳好，近黄昏；朝阳美，向上进。
过这村，没这店；不奉献，待何年？
把最美，献最爱！人一生，最开怀！
把最好，给最需；人一生，最有义！

译文

有了好钢，要放在刀刃上；有了好粉，要涂在脸上。
有了吃穿，要奔向安康；有了真正，要把善美去创。
人生几十年，转眼就离去；你要留下什么，奉献给这里？
别光说，我爱你！你的真善美，在哪里？
夕阳无限好，只是近黄昏；朝阳无限美，只有向上进。
过了这村，没有这店；你不奉献，等待到何年？
把最美的，奉献给自己最爱的！在人的一生中，是最开怀的！
把最好的，奉献给最需要的！在人的一生中，是最有意义的！

《一二三》

（9）好社会（119）

好社会，慢慢现；讲诚信，重良环。
从被动，到主动；从分摊，到自愿。
有付出，有得到；股份制，最美妙！
福同享，难同当；踏实地，创辉煌。
前植树，后乘凉；滴水恩，永不忘。
取于民，用于民；用良心，做美人。
人自控，物自动；无为治，得大同！

译文

好的社会，慢慢出现；讲究诚信，重视良环。
从被动去做，到主动去做；从分摊责任，到自愿承担。
有了付出，就有得到；股份制度，最为美妙！
有福同享，有难同当；脚踏实地，创造辉煌。
前人植树，后人乘凉；滴水之恩，永不相忘。
取之于民，用之于民；要用良心，去做美人。
人能自控，物能自动；无为而治，得到大同！

（10）核心观（120）

核心观，　24言；人人爱，处处传。
强民主，明和谐；由平等，正法制。
国敬业，信友善；创善美，向高远！
五原则，是道德；周恩来，赛诸葛。
尊主权，土完整；不侵犯，不干政。
平互利，和共处；真正创，保安康！
民做主，权分立；群龙起，谁能比？
青藏高，江河远；昨今慧，明无限！

译文

核心观念，24之言；人人喜欢，个个相传。
富强民主，文明和谐；自由平等，公正法治。
爱国敬业，诚信友善；创造善美，走向高远！
五项原则，是国家间的道德规则；周恩来的能力，超越了诸葛亮。
互相尊重主权和领土完整；互不侵犯，互不干涉内政。
平等互利，和平共处；真正地创造，才能确保安全健康！
人民做主，权力分立；群龙而起，谁能相比？
青藏高原高，长江黄河水流远；昨今智慧，明天无限！

《一二三》

（11）想什么（121）

想什么？做什么？找问题！解问惑！
人活着，为什么？为传承，为吃乐！
吃乐寿，低中求；活万年，终要走。
传人文，是根本！最长远，最高深！
没有人，何来文？无人文，何来魂？
真正创，善美文；助我们，向前进。
做阶梯，做桥梁；为梦想，仁不让！
去匆匆，来匆匆；怎样做，最真正？

译文

要想什么？要做什么？寻找问题！解决问题和疑惑！
人活着，为了什么？为了传承，为了吃乐！
吃喝快乐长寿，是低级和中级的追求；即使能活万年，最终也要走。
传承人和文化，是最根本的事情！是最长远的，是最高深的！
没有人，从哪里来文化？没有人和文化，从哪里来灵魂？
真正创善美的文化；能够帮助我们向前进。
我们要做阶梯，我们要做桥梁；为了梦想，当仁不让！
去也匆匆，来也匆匆；怎样去做，才能最真正？

第五章

（12）万代传（122）

人物它，成系统；要和谐，动态衡。
吃安真，要稳展；多位体，在循环。
创消费，生死关！源有限，必节俭！
一个人，一天三；数亿人，惊地天。
假歪费，若超限；系统乱，成灾难。
死安乐，生忧患！无远忧，必近患！
家千口，能人担！国亿家，真正管！
提素质，顺自然！控人口，万代传！

译文

人，动植物和其他物，构成系统；要想和谐，就要动态平衡。

吃穿住行，安康福乐和真正创善，需要，稳定与发展；多位一体，正在循环。

创造与消费，生死攸关！资源有限，必须节俭！

一个人，一天三顿饭；数亿的人，光饭的数量就惊动地天。

虚假，不正和浪费，如果超过了限度；系统就会混乱，最后酿成灾难。

死于安乐，生于忧患！没有远忧，必有近患！

家有多人，有能之人，担当重任！国有数亿之家，必须真正地去管理！

提高素质，顺应自然！合理地控制人口，才能万代相传！

《一二三》

（13）三百千（123）

《三百千》，《弟子规》；《一二三》，承前飞。
　请给我，真机会；我要去，奉献美！
　各家姓，立学会；互帮学，向善美。
　万家姓，万家会；竞发展，共腾飞。
　一二三，基金会；让世界，变更美。
　诺贝尔，一二三；东西方，竞向前。
　一二三，养生园；你我他，共创建。
　想筹做，步步艰；正果敢，胜今天！
　是真星，不怕炼；要发光，照无限。
　好真正，美创善：人生航，《一二三》！

译文

《三百千》，《弟子规》；《一二三》，继承前人的成果，向前向上飞。

请给我，真正的机会！我要去奉献，真正创善美！

各个姓氏，都要成立学会；互帮互学，走向善美。

数万家姓氏，数万家学会；竞争发展，共同腾飞。

一二三，基金会的成立；会让世界，变得更美。

诺贝尔奖金，一二三奖金；东西方，要良性竞争，向前发展。

要建设，一二三，养生园；你我他，共同去创建。

思想，筹划和实际去做，步步艰难！正确，果断和勇敢，胜利就在今天！

真正的恒星，是不怕火炼的；需要发光，照亮无限。

好的真正，美的创善：人生导航，《一二三》！

www.ingramcontent.com/pod-product-compliance
Lightning Source LLC
Chambersburg PA
CBHW060834190426
43197CB00039B/2607